en español

Rapid Success in Spanish for Beginners

Language Immersion Institute Series

en español

Rapid Success in Spanish for Beginners

Graciela España

Series Editor: Professor Henry Urbanski, Ph.D.
State University of New York at New Paltz

McGraw·Hill

New York   Chicago   San Francisco   Lisbon   London   Madrid   Mexico City
Milan   New Delhi   San Juan   Seoul   Singapore   Sydney   Toronto

Library of Congress Cataloging-in-Publication Data

España, Graciela.
    En español : rapid success in Spanish for beginners / Graciela España.
      p.   cm.
    ISBN 0-07-140643-3 (bk. : alk. paper) — ISBN 0-07-140642-5 (package)

    1. Spanish language—Conversation and phrase books—English. I. Title.

PC4121 .E74 2002
468.3′421—dc21   2002035353

1 2 3 4 5 6 7 8 9 0   AGM/AGM   2 1 0 9 8 7 6 5 4 3

Package ISBN 0-07-140642-5
Book ISBN 0-07-140643-3

In the same series:
En français, Marc Bendali and Marie-Paule Mahoney (lead authorial team)
In italiano, Sandra Immerso

McGraw-Hill books are available at special quantity discounts to use as premiums and
sales promotions, or for use in corporate training programs. For more information, please
write to the Director of Special Sales, Professional Publishing, McGraw-Hill, Two Penn
Plaza, New York, NY 10121-2298. Or contact your local bookstore.

This book is printed on acid-free paper.

Contents

Introduction   vii

How to use this course   ix

En camino · *On the way*   1

DIALOG 1   Nuevos amigos · *New friends*   2

DIALOG 2   Presentaciones · *Introductions*   6

¡Me gusta aprender! · *I like to learn!*   17

DIALOG 1   Hasta pronto · *See you soon*   18

DIALOG 2   ¡Me gusta ____! · *I like ____!*   22

¡Me encanta este capítulo! · *I love this chapter!*   30

DIALOG 1   ¡Me encanta ____! · *I love ____!*   31

DIALOG 2   ¡Me encanta practicar! · *I love to practice!*   37

De viaje · *On a trip*   46

DIALOG 1   Haciendo las maletas · *Packing*   47

DIALOG 2   En el aeropuerto · *At the airport*   51

5

Llegando al hotel · *Arriving at the hotel*   58

DIALOG 1   En un taxi · *In a taxi*   59

DIALOG 2   En el hotel · *At the hotel*   64

DIALOG 3   Quisiera hacer una reservación · *I would like to make a reservation*   71

◄ **6** ►

En el hotel · *At the hotel*   74

DIALOG 1   La habitación · *The room*   75

DIALOG 2   ¡Te quiero! · *I love you!*   80

DIALOG 3   ¿Me puede ___? · *Can you ___ for me?*   83

◄ **7** ►

En el restaurante · *At the restaurant*   89

DIALOG 1   ¿Qué desean pedir? · *What would you like to have?*   90

DIALOG 2   ¿Qué desean comer? · *What would you like to eat?*   98

DIALOG 3   ¿Dejamos propina? · *Do we leave a tip?*   103

◄ **8** ►

Por la ciudad · *Around the city*   108

DIALOG 1   México D.F. · *Mexico City*   109

DIALOG 2   Vamos a las pirámides · *Let's go to the pyramids*   116

DIALOG 3   Descansando en Acapulco · *Resting in Acapulco*   122

◄ **9** ►

Lo pasamos muy bien · *We had a great time*   130

DIALOG 1   ¡Fuimos a Oaxaca! · *We went to Oaxaca!*   131

DIALOG 2   Nos perdimos, pero... · *We got lost, but . . .*   137

DIALOG 3   De vuelta · *Going back*   144

Answer key   149

Grammar summary   157

Spanish-English glossary   165

English-Spanish glossary   174

Introduction

Since 1981 the Language Immersion Institute, located at the State University of New York at New Paltz, has provided foreign language courses for more than 40,000 participants from all walks of life. The Institute's purpose has always been to proliferate foreign language study among adult learners through creative methods and programs that complement their busy work schedules and help them acquire proficiency in the shortest time possible.

The Immersion approach is predicated on the idea that intensive language study creates a highly effective and exciting learning environment that is congenial and non-threatening, and in which confidence in speaking ability is quickly attained. This is especially important in our rapidly shrinking world, where communication skills are vital. In the context of the global village we have become, the Language Immersion Institute offers innovative ways to study foreign languages, including English as a Second Language.

The mission of the Language Immersion Institute is threefold:

1. To make language study accessible and convenient to the adult learner through intensive courses that provide survival skills and practical conversational skills at all levels, thereby addressing the needs of persons beyond the secondary school level.

2. To dispel the misconception that language learning is a formidable task by dividing the learning process into small, progressive modules in which the learner discovers that acquiring language skills can be an achievable goal and an enjoyable endeavor.

3. To provide a real-life learning environment, in addition to the classroom, through overseas courses and other off-campus classes that stimulate the learner to use the language in a natural, non-academic setting.

This course series, including *En español*, is one way the Institute strives to bring foreign language study to the adult learner. Written by native-speaking teachers with many years of experience teaching at the Language Immersion Institute, the programs cover Elementary Levels I and II, the equivalent of six weekend courses or two semesters of study. As important as content, the programs also reflect the spirit of classes at the Language Immersion Institute. The audio recordings, a key component of the courses, were recorded in New Paltz by Institute teachers—not actors—to convey the infectious vitality that imbues the classes at the LII.

I hope you find studying Spanish with this program a rewarding and inspiring experience.

Professor Henry Urbanski
Distinguished Service Professor of Russian,
Founder and Director of the Language Immersion Institute

How to use this course

This course is designed to help you master speaking Spanish in real-life situations by learning vocabulary in context, basic grammar, and helpful cultural information.

The course is presented in nine chapters. Each chapter contains two or three dialogs, followed by a list of new vocabulary (**Vocabulario**) used in the dialog and additional vocabulary (**Vocabulario adicional**) related to the subject presented, but not used in the dialog. Each dialog introduces new expressions or structures, as well as new vocabulary used in context. To help you understand these new expressions, explanations of grammar (**Estructura gramatical**) or structure (**Comprensión y expresión**) are provided. Written exercises in this book and audio exercises on the CD offer ample opportunity to practice the material. As an optional aid, the text of the audio practices and the audio exercise questions is included in the book. This way you will hear, repeat, and write the new structures until you master them.

Most chapters contain a section called **Pitfall**, where you will hear a student and teacher interact on the recording. This section is intended to help you review the new material and to show you some typical mistakes to avoid. Also on the recording, the section called **Expresión libre** poses questions to be answered as in a spontaneous conversation. Returning to this book, ¡**Viva la diferencia!** provides cultural information that will help you understand the language from a personal perspective. Finally, at the end of each chapter, **How to make it sound Spanish** will help you master pronunciation.

At the back of the book is the **Answer key**, where you will find the solution for each written exercise (answers to audio exercises are on the recording), so you can be sure at all times that you know the right answer. The **Grammar summary** is a synopsis of selected grammatical aspects covered in the program for quick reference. And the **Spanish-English glossary** and **English-Spanish glossary** allow you to find the Spanish or English equivalents of all the vocabulary presented.

To benefit the most from this course, you should follow certain steps.

1. Begin each section by listening to the dialog and repeating after the speaker.
2. Read the dialog with the help of the vocabulary list following the dialog.
3. Study the grammatical or structural explanations and examples.
4. Practice with the CD, listening and repeating aloud.
5. Answer the questions and complete the oral and written exercises.
6. Make sure your answers are correct by checking the answer key.
7. Go back and review the material whenever something is not clear or you do not remember. When learning a language it is very important to have a firm basis on which to continue.

In order to understand and retain the material, the following approach is suggested.

1. Open your book to the beginning of the chapter you are about to study. Read the chapter's objective and insert the CD.
2. Listen to the first dialog, then stop the recording.
3. Read the dialog in the book, looking up the words you don't know in the Vocabulary section. Study the new vocabulary before you proceed.
4. Replay the dialog, pausing the CD to allow you to repeat each segment. Repeat this as many times as necessary to both recognize the vocabulary and pronounce the words clearly and with ease.
5. Following the instructions on the CD or in the book, progress through the grammatical explanations and the exercises in the book and on the CD until you come to the next dialog.

    It is important to work at your own pace and take all the time you need to practice. Do not proceed to the next exercise until you feel you have mastered the one you just completed. Going over an audio exercise as many times as necessary is the key to progress. Also, try to imitate the speakers' intonation and pronunciation as closely as possible.
6. Once you have mastered the vocabulary and the exercises, move on to the next dialog and repeat steps one to five.

¡Buena suerte! (Good luck!)

◄ 1 ►

En camino
On the way

OBJECTIVE

In this chapter you will learn how to greet and introduce yourself to others, and how to ask someone's
name in Spanish. You will also learn to ask and state
someone's profession or nationality, and to say where
someone is from. After some practice you will be
amazed to discover that saying today's date, telling
where you are from, or giving your full address in Spanish is not as difficult as you may have thought.

In the first dialog you will meet David Wood, who is
taking a Spanish course at the Language Immersion
Institute at New Paltz. In the course of this book, he
is going to travel to Mexico with his wife, Anita. Listen
to him and the people he meets.

◄ **1.1** ►

DIALOG 1
Nuevos amigos · *New friends*

Two people are talking before the Spanish classes begin at the
Immersion Institute in New Paltz. Let's meet David Wood and
José Naveas, two Americans who have come to the Institute to
study Spanish. Their first encounter is very brief, however, since
José is in a hurry to go somewhere.

Dos personas conversan en el Instituto de Inmersión. David y José
son dos estudiantes americanos del Instituto de Inmersión en New
Paltz.

DAVID	¡Buenos días! ¿Cómo estás?
JOSÉ	Muy bien, gracias. ¿Y tú?
DAVID	Bien, gracias. Me llamo David Wood, ¿cómo te llamas?
JOSÉ	Me llamo José Naveas. Perdón, tengo prisa.
DAVID	Adiós, hasta pronto.

◄ **1.2** ►

Vocabulario

dos personas conversan	*two people are talking*
en el Instituto de Inmersión	*at the Immersion Institute*
son dos estudiantes americanos	*they are two American students*
buenos días	*good morning*
¿Cómo estás?	*How are you?*
muy bien, gracias	*very well, thanks*
me llamo _____	*my name is* _____
¿Cómo te llamas?	*What is your name?*
perdón	*excuse me*
tengo prisa	*I am in a hurry*
adiós	*good-bye*
hasta pronto	*see you soon*

Vocabulario adicional

el amigo	*male friend*
la amiga	*female friend*

Expresiones idiomáticas

perdón	*excuse me*
perdóneme	*forgive me*
¿Cómo te llamas?	*What is your name?*

◄ 1.3 ►
Audio practice

On the recording, practice greeting people according to the time of day.

Buenos días.	(in the morning)
Buenos días, señor.	
Buenos días, señor González.	
Buenos días, señora.	
Buenos días, señora Ramos.	
Buenos días, señorita Campos.	

Buenas tardes.	(in the afternoon or evening)
Buenas tardes, señor Ramírez.	
Buenas tardes, señora Olmos.	
Buenas tardes, señorita Gutiérrez.	

Buenos días, señores.	(greeting more than one person)
Buenos días, señoras.	
Buenas tardes, señoritas.	
Buenos días, señoras y señores.	

Buenas noches.	(toward the end of the day)
Buenas noches, Carlos.	
Buenas noches, señora Aguilera.	
Buenas noches, señorita Colón.	
Buenas noches, señores.	
Buenas noches, señoras.	
Buenas noches, señoras y señores.	

◄ 1.4 ►
Comprensión y expresión

Greetings

In Spanish, ways of greeting depend on the time of day. **Buenos días** is appropriate in the morning, and **Buenas tardes** from midday to 7 P.M. After 7 P.M. we use **Buenas noches** as a greeting and as a farewell.

When talking to someone you do not know very well, you should add a title of respect to your greeting.

señor	*for a man*
señora	*for an older or married woman*
señorita	*for a young, unmarried woman or a girl*

If you are talking to more than one person, you will use **señoras** for a group of women, **señoritas** for a group of young women, and **señores** for a group of men or a mixed group.

Buenos días, señoras.
Buenas tardes, señoritas.
Buenas noches, señores.

You may add **¿Cómo está?**, which means "How are you?" in a formal greeting. In a somewhat informal greeting you ask **¿Cómo estás? Está** is the formal word for "you are." **Estás** is the informal word.

Hola is the most informal greeting. It is used at any time of day.

¡Hola, Carolina! ¿Qué tal?

So if you are talking to a friend or someone your age or of your social status, you may say **¿Cómo estás?** or **¿Qué tal?**, which means "How are things?"

There are several phrases you may use to answer the question "How are you?"

muy bien, gracias	*very well, thank you*
bien, gracias	*well, thank you*
más o menos	*so-so*
mal	*bad*
muy mal	*very bad*

Saying good-bye

Here are some phrases you may use when you need to say good-bye.

hasta luego	*see you later*
hasta pronto	*see you soon*
hasta mañana	*see you tomorrow*

hasta la vista	*till I see you*
hasta el sábado	*till Saturday*
adiós	*good-bye*
chao	*good-bye (informal)*

◄ 1.5 ►
Audio exercise

Listen to the recording as you look at the pictures below. Using their proper names, greet the different people according to the time of the day. Then repeat the correct answer after the speaker.

EXAMPLE   ¡Buenas noches, señor!

1.   2.   3.

4.   5.   6.

◄ 1.6 ►
Audio practice

yamas

When you want to ask someone's name in an informal situation, the question is **¿Cómo te llamas?**, literally "What do you call yourself?" When you need to be formal, the question is **¿Cómo se llama usted?** The reply is **Me llamo**, followed by your name. Practice this on the recording.   *y yarmo*

◄ **1.7** ►
Audio exercise

Listen to the recording as you look at the pictures below. Pretend that you are each of these people, and answer the question **¿Cómo te llamas?** or **¿Cómo se llama usted?** by replying **Me llamo**, followed by the appropriate name.

1. Clara Gómez

2. Ricardo Morales

3. Juan Hernández

4. Pedro Villa

5. Isabel Delgado

6. Miguel Espinoza

 ◄ **1.8** ►
DIALOG 2
Presentaciones · *Introductions*

Later, David again meets José, who is talking to a young woman. José introduces David to the woman, whose name is Cecilia. An introduction (**Te presento a** _____) is generally followed by **Mucho gusto** or **Encantado(-a)** ("delighted"). Notice the way José introduces Cecilia to David.

Cuando David y José se encuentran otra vez, José está hablando con una señorita; José se la presenta a David.

DAVID   ¿Qué tal, José?

JOSÉ   Hola, David. Te presento a Cecilia Magdalena Egaña Leal.

DAVID   Mucho gusto, Cecilia.

CECILIA   El gusto es mío. ¿De dónde eres, David?
DAVID   Soy de los Estados Unidos, de Nueva York. ¿Y tú?
CECILIA   Soy de Ecuador, de Quito.
JOSÉ   Y yo soy de California. Mis padres son de México.

◄ 1.9 ►
Vocabulario

se encuentran	*they meet*
está hablando	*he is talking*
se la presenta	*he introduces her*
¿Qué tal?	*How are things?*
Hola	*Hi*
Te presento a _____	*I'd like you to meet _____*
mucho gusto	*my pleasure*
El gusto es mío.	*The pleasure is mine.*
¿De dónde eres?	*Where are you from?*
Soy de _____	*I am from _____*
¿Y tú?	*And you?*
mis padres son	*my parents are*

Vocabulario adicional

encantado(-a)	*delighted*

◄ 1.10 ►
Comprensión y expresión

Introductions

When we need to introduce someone, we say **Te presento a** _____, followed by the name of the person being introduced. The answer is **Mucho gusto**. The person being introduced responds with **El gusto es mío** or simply **Mucho gusto**.

In the following example, María introduces Dr. Ramos to her friend Elena.

MARÍA   Elena, te presento a la doctora Ramos.
ELENA   Mucho gusto, Dra. Ramos.
DRA. RAMOS   El gusto es mío.

Asking where someone is from

When we want to know where someone is from, we ask ¿De dónde eres? The answer is Soy de _____ ("I am from _____"), followed by the city or town, or country of origin. When we need to be formal, for instance, when we are talking to an older person, the question is ¿De dónde es usted? In the dialog below, two young students are talking at the university on their first day of classes, so they use the informal ¿De dónde eres?

In the following example, Carlos is talking to someone he has just met.

CARLOS   ¿De dónde eres?
MAURICIO   Soy de Argentina, ¿y tú?
CARLOS   Soy de Puerto Rico.

Insert the CD to practice more greetings.

◄ 1.11 ►
Estructura gramatical

On the recording, try to hear the difference in the pronunciation of the last syllable of the adjective **americano** and the feminine form **americana**.

David es americano. OR Él es americano.
Anita es americana. OR Ella es americana.

El señor Wood es americano. OR Él es americano.
La señora Wood es americana. OR Ella es americana.
Los señores Wood son americanos. OR Ellos son
   americanos.
Mary y Lisa son americanas. OR Ellas son americanas.

Es and **son** are two forms of the verb **ser** ("to be"). Here are all the forms of this verb.

yo soy	*I am*
tú eres	*you (singular, familiar) are*
él es	*he is*
ella es	*she is*
usted es	*you (singular, formal) are*

nosotros somos	*we are*
ellos son	*they (males, or males and females) are*
ellas son	*they (females) are*
ustedes son	*you (plural) are*

Notice that in Spanish the "you" form can be informal, **tú**, when talking to friends or members of your family; or it can be formal, **usted**, when talking to people you don't know well or someone you need to address formally. The abbreviation for **usted** is **Ud.**

In Spain and some other Spanish-speaking areas, **vosotros** or **vosotras** is generally used to express the plural "you." This form, however, will not be used in this book.

To say what a person's profession is, you add the profession directly after the form of the verb **ser.**

Juan es abogado. OR Él es abogado.
He is a lawyer.
María es periodista. OR Ella es periodista.
She is a journalist.

To say what someone's nationality is, you add the nationality directly after the form of the verb **ser.**

Rosa y Ana son cubanas. OR Ellas son cubanas.
They are Cuban.
Carlos y yo somos chilenos. OR Nosotros somos chilenos.
We are Chilean.

To ask where someone is from, the question is **¿De dónde?** followed by the proper form of **ser.**

| MARÍA | ¿De dónde eres? | *Where are you from?* |
| CARLOS | Soy de Argentina. | *I am from Argentina.* |

Notice that in Spanish you do not need to use the personal pronouns. You may say **yo soy** or simply **soy.** Also notice that when you ask a question in Spanish, you raise the intonation of your voice at the end of the question.

| CARLOS | ¿De dónde es Catalina? | *Where is Catalina from?* |
| MARÍA | Es de Madrid. | *She is from Madrid.* |

 Insert the CD to practice saying where people are from, using the verb **ser.**

◄ **1.12** ►

Audio exercise

Imagine you are on a cruise in South America and you try to introduce yourself to some of the other passengers. You will be the person depicted in each picture below. On the recording, you will be asked your name and where you are from. Answer the questions and add your profession.

1. Clara Gómez, Santo Domingo, abogada

2. Ricardo Morales, Barcelona, doctor

3. Juan Hernández, Santiago, estudiante

4. Pedro Villa, Colombia, periodista

5. Isabel Delgado, Los Angeles, actriz

6. Miguel Espinoza, Buenos Aires, estudiante

◄ 1.13 ►
Audio exercise

On the recording, practice greeting people according to the time of day using **Buenos días** or **Buenas tardes** and adding **señorita**, **señora**, **señor**, or the plural form **señoritas**, **señoras**, or **señores**. Use **señores** for a mixed group of men and women.

EXAMPLE   It's 7 A.M. when Carlos meets señora Galindo.

CARLOS   Buenos días, señora.

◄ 1.14 ►
Pitfall

No muy bueno, sino muy bien · *Not very good, but very well*

Review some of the greetings you have just learned by listening to a conversation on the recording between a student and a teacher at the Immersion Institute. Pay attention to the mistakes the student makes and how they are corrected.

John forgets the meaning of **¿Qué tal?**, but the teacher helps him remember by both repeating the question and saying the other greeting, **¿Cómo estás?** Unfortunately, John becomes a bit nervous and answers **Muy bueno**, which means "very good," instead of answering "very well," which in Spanish is **Muy bien**. Anybody can make a mistake; the important thing is to learn from it.

◄ 1.15 ►
Exercise

Complete the following sentences with the correct verb form.

EXAMPLE   Yo _soy_ americano.

1. El _____ profesor.

2. Nosotros _____ colombianos.

3. Usted _____ peruana.

4. Yo _____ abogada.

5. Marcos y María Luisa _____ inteligentes.

6. Tú _____ mexicano.

7. Matilde y Carolina _____ recepcionistas.

8. La señora Vásquez _____ simpática.

◄ 1.16 ►
Exercise

Complete the following sentences with the correct pronoun.

EXAMPLE   _Yo_ soy artista.

1. _____ eres chileno.

2. _____ es profesora.

3. _____ somos venezolanos.

4. _____ soy de Costa Rica.

5. _____ son americanas.

6. _____ es doctor.

◄ 1.17 ►
Exercise

Answer the following questions using the personal pronoun and the proper form of **ser**.

EXAMPLE   ¿El presidente Bush es americano?

Sí, él es americano.

1. ¿Los amigos son de Bogotá?

   _____

2. ¿Juan es jugador de tenis?

   _____

3. ¿Eres americano?

   _____

4. ¿Somos de China?

   _____

5. ¿Ustedes son arquitectos?

   _____

6. ¿Plácido Domingo es de España?

   _____

◄ **1.18** ►
Exercise

Most names of professions are very similar in Spanish and English. See if you can identify the following ones. Write the equivalent word in English.

1. doctor   _____

2. recepcionista   _____

3. veterinario   _____

4. plomero   _____

5. profesor   _____

6. mecánico   _____

7. dentista   _____

8. electricista   _____

9. secretario   _____

10. arquitecto   _____

 ◄ **1.19** ►
Audio exercise

Using the appropriate pronoun (**él**, **ellas**, etc.) and verb form (**es**, **son**, etc.), give the profession of the following characters. The speaker will give you the correct answer after the pause.

1. Dra. Gloria Paredes, veterinaria

2. Ricardo Morales, doctor

3. Mario Gamboa, Pedro Bedoya, mecánicos

4. Pedro Villa, periodista

5. Dra. Valeria Suazo, Dra. Olivia Carrasco, dentistas

6. Miguel Espinoza, estudiante

◄ **1.20** ►
Exercise

Select the appropriate adjective of nationality and complete the following sentences.

italiano   chino   puertorriqueño   argentina   canadiense
inglesa   cubano   franceses   español   mexicana

1. La princesa Diana es _____.

2. Edith Piaf y Charles de Gaulle son _____.

3. Ricky Martin es _____.

4. Salvador Dalí es _____.

5. Leonardo da Vinci es _____.

6. Evita Perón es _____.

7. Mao Tsé Tung es _____.

8. Fidel Castro es _____.

◄ **1.21** ►
Expresión libre

Using what you have learned in this chapter, listen to the recording and take part in a spontaneous conversation. This will review your ability to make introductions and say your name, nationality, and home city.

◄ 1.22 ►
¡Viva la diferencia!

- In Spanish-speaking countries, people use two last names (and frequently two given names also)—for example, Cecilia Magdalena Egaña Leal. Egaña is her father's family name; Leal is her mother's family name. She is addressed as Miss Egaña, or Miss Egaña Leal. Her friends call her Cecilia Magdalena, Cecilia, or Ceci.

- In Spanish, a person's title is used as a sign of respect.

señor (Sr.)	*Mr.*	doctor (Dr.)	*doctor*
señora (Sra.)	*Mrs.*	doctora (Dra.)	*female doctor*
señorita (Srta.)	*Miss*		

- Here is a list of Spanish-speaking countries.

COUNTRY	CAPITAL	NATIONALITY
Argentina	Buenos Aires	argentino(-a)
Bolivia	La Paz	boliviano(-a)
Chile	Santiago	chileno(-a)
Colombia	Bogotá	colombiano(-a)
Costa Rica	San José	costarricense
Cuba	La Habana	cubano(-a)
Ecuador	Quito	ecuatoriano(-a)
España	Madrid	español, española
Guatemala	Ciudad de Guatemala	guatemalteco(-a)
Honduras	Tegucigalpa	hondureño(-a)
México	México D.F.	mexicano(-a)
Panamá	Ciudad de Panamá	panameño(-a)
Paraguay	Asunción	paraguayo(-a)
Perú	Lima	peruano(-a)
Puerto Rico	San Juan	puertorriqueño(-a)
República Dominicana	Santo Domingo	dominicano(-a)
Uruguay	Montevideo	uruguayo(-a)
Venezuela	Caracas	venezolano(-a)

Notice that the nationality must agree with the gender and number of the people or objects it refers to.

María es argentina.
Juan y Pedro son argentinos.

◄ **1.23** ►

How to make it sound Spanish

Spanish has five distinctive sounds, the sounds of the five vowels: **a, e, i, o, u**. These sounds do not vary, no matter where the vowels are located in a word. For instance, the vowel **a** sounds the same in **Ana, mamá, cámara**, etc.

a   has a clear sound, such as in the word "America": **adiós, arquitecto, Argentina**

e   is similar to the sound **e** in "get": **ese, elemento, mete**

i   is similar to the **i** in the word "police": **si, ni, límite**

o   is similar to the **o** in "old": **coro, loro, oso**

u   is pronounced as the **oo** in "boot": **luna, cuna, uno**

◄ 2 ►

¡Me gusta aprender!
I like to learn!

OBJECTIVE

In this chapter you will learn how to say an address, a telephone number, and a date. To do so you will learn the months, days, and numbers up to 100. You will also learn how to express preferences ("I like" or "I love") and how to use the definite articles. At the same time you will acquire vocabulary related to professions and occupations.

◄ **2.1** ►
DIALOG 1
Hasta pronto · *See you soon*

Adiós is commonly used in the Hispanic world to say good-bye. However, it is usually used when we leave somebody for a long time or forever. When we want to say good-bye, we say **hasta pronto**, **hasta mañana**, **hasta luego**, and so on. Nevertheless, although we hope that David and José are going to see each other again soon, in the following dialog after classes have finished for the day, they say **adiós** and exchange addresses and phone numbers.

Después de clases, David y José hablan otra vez.

DAVID   Voy a México con mi esposa en octubre.

JOSÉ   ¡Ah! ¡Eres casado! Yo soy soltero. ¿Por qué vas a México?

DAVID   Necesito hacer una entrevista en la Ciudad de México. Soy periodista y mi esposa es abogada.

JOSÉ   Pues, yo soy profesor de literatura inglesa en una universidad.

DAVID   ¿Cuál es tu dirección?

JOSÉ   Vivo en la calle 18 número 40, apartamento 3C, Nueva York, NY 10028 (Calle 18 Nº 40, Apt. 3C). ¿Cuál es tu número de teléfono?

DAVID   Mi número de teléfono es código de área 718, número 555-4596.

JOSÉ   Muchas gracias y adiós.

DAVID   ¡Hasta pronto!

◄ **2.2** ►
Vocabulario

después de clases	*after classes*
hablan	*they speak*
otra vez	*again*
voy a	*I am going to*
con mi esposa	*with my wife*
casado(-a)	*married*
soltero(-a)	*single*
¿por qué?	*why?*
vas	*you are going*

necesito	*I need*
hacer	*to do, to make*
una entrevista	*an interview*
la ciudad de	*the city of*
el/la periodista	*journalist*
el profesor/la profesora	*professor, teacher*
la literatura inglesa	*English literature*
el abogado/la abogada	*lawyer*
la universidad	*university*
¿Cuál es tu dirección?	*What is your address?*
el número de teléfono	*phone number*
vivo	*I live*
la calle	*street*
el apartamento	*apartment*
el código de área	*area code*
¿cuál?	*which?*
Hasta pronto.	*See you soon.*

Vocabulario adicional

el viudo/la viuda	*widower, widow*
separado(-a)	*separated*
divorciado(-a)	*divorced*
repita por favor	*please repeat*

Profesiones y ocupaciones

el arquitecto/la arquitecta	*architect*
el ingeniero/la ingeniera	*engineer*
el actor/la actriz	*actor, actress*
el/la dentista	*dentist*
el plomero/la plomera	*plumber*
el cocinero/la cocinera	*cook*
el peluquero/la peluquera	*hairdresser*
el/la cantante	*singer*
el/la artista	*artist*
el/la agente de bienes raíces	*real estate agent*
el/la agente de seguros	*insurance agent*
el locutor/la locutora	*TV and radio announcer*
el mozo, el camarero/ la camarera	*waiter, waitress*

◄ **2.3** ►
Audio practice

Let's look at how José gives his street address to David.

DAVID	¿Cuál es tu dirección?
JOSÉ	Calle dieciocho.
DAVID	¿Número?
JOSÉ	Número cuarenta.
DAVID	¿Apartamento?
JOSÉ	Apartamento tres C (Ce).
DAVID	¿Nueva York?
JOSÉ	Sí, Nueva York.

To give an address you need to use numbers. Here's a song that will help you learn some of them.

Dos y dos son cuatro,	2 + 2 = 4
Cuatro y dos son seis,	4 + 2 = 6
Seis y dos son ocho,	6 + 2 = 8
Y ocho, dieciséis,	+ 8 (=) 16
Y ocho, veinticuatro,	+ 8 (=) 24
Y ocho, treinta y dos,	+ 8 (=) 32
Y ocho, son cuarenta,	+ 8 (=) 40
Y ya se acabó.	*and that's all.*

That is a nice song, but some numbers are missing. In case you don't know how to say the numbers one to ten, here they are.

uno	1	seis	6
dos	2	siete	7
tres	3	ocho	8
cuatro	4	nueve	9
cinco	5	diez	10

The Spanish for zero is **cero**. And here are the numbers in tens.

diez	10	sesenta	60
veinte	20	setenta	70
treinta	30	ochenta	80
cuarenta	40	noventa	90
cincuenta	50	cien	100

◄ 2.4 ►
Comprensión y expresión

Saying your address

One way to ask for someone's address in Spanish is to say **¿Cuál es tu dirección?** ("What is your address?")

MARÍA   ¿Cuál es tu dirección?
ELENA   Calle Teatinos número 36, apartamento 11, Santiago.

Notice that the address begins with **Calle** or **Avenida**, followed by the building or house number. This is a bit different from English.

Sometimes, when the address is long and we do not catch all the information at once, we may say **¿Número?**, **¿Apartamento?**, and so on.

Saying your phone number

To ask for a phone number, we say **¿Cuál es tu número de teléfono?** In writing, we usually abbreviate the word **número** as **Nº**.

MARÍA   ¿Cuál es tu número de teléfono?
ELENA   Mi número de teléfono es 495-3701
       (spoken 4-95-37-01, **cuatro, noventa y cinco, treinta y siete, cero uno**).

Notice that, in Spanish, spoken telephone numbers are grouped in pairs.

 Listen to the recording to practice saying your address and your telephone number. Then write the phone numbers in digits.

1. _____   2. _____   3. _____

◄ 2.5 ►
Exercise

Write out the following telephone numbers as they would be said in Spanish.

1. (618) 476-5123

2. (212) 270-0366

_____

3. (413) 772-8945

_____

◄ 2.6 ►
DIALOG 2
¡Me gusta _____! · *I like _____!*

The next day of classes the two new friends are together again. David tells José that he and his wife are going to Mexico in October. José is going there for Christmas vacation. Listen to their conversation.

David y José hablan de la clase de español. David va a México en octubre y José va en diciembre.

DAVID	¿Qué tal la clase de español?
JOSÉ	¡Ah! Me encanta la clase de español. Mira, usamos este libro.
DAVID	Me gusta mucho mi clase también. La profesora es muy simpática. ¿Sabes? Mi esposa y yo vamos a México el ocho de octubre.
JOSÉ	¡Qué bueno! Yo voy a México en diciembre para las vacaciones de Navidad.

◄ 2.7 ►
Vocabulario

¿Qué tal tu clase?	*How is your class?*
me encanta	*I love*
mira	*look*
Usamos este libro.	*We use this book.*
me gusta mucho	*I like very much*
simpática	*nice*
¿Sabes?	*You know?*
mi esposa	*my wife*
vamos	*we are going*
¡Qué bueno!	*Great! (literally, "how good")*
para las vacaciones	*for vacation*
Navidad	*Christmas*

Vocabulario adicional

el escritorio	*desk*
la calculadora	*calculator*
el cuaderno	*notebook*
el casete	*cassette*
la clase	*class*
la carpeta	*binder, folder*
el lápiz	*pencil*
la hoja de papel	*sheet of paper*
mucho	*very much*

Expresiones idiomáticas

The expression **¿Qué tal?** is used both as a greeting and as a question meaning **How is** _____? That is why David asks **¿Qué tal la clase de español?**

◄ 2.8 ►

Comprensión y expresión

Saying you like someone or something

In Spanish, when you want to say that you like someone or something, you say **me gusta**. When you are more enthusiastic and you want to say that you love something, you say **me encanta**. Listen to the recording to practice these phrases.

¿Te gusta la clase?	*Do you like class?*
¡Me encanta la clase!	*I love class!*
¿Te gusta el libro?	*Do you like the book?*
Sí, me gusta el libro.	*Yes, I like the book.*
¿Te gusta el casete?	*Do you like the tape?*
Sí, ¡me gusta mucho!	*Yes, I like it a lot!*

Months of the year

If you want to ask what is the current month, the question is **¿En qué mes estamos?**

DAVID	¿En qué mes estamos?
CECILIA	Estamos en septiembre.

Here are all the months of the year.

enero	*January*
febrero	*February*
marzo	*March*
abril	*April*
mayo	*May*
junio	*June*
julio	*July*
agosto	*August*
septiembre	*September*
octubre	*October*
noviembre	*November*
diciembre	*December*

Spaniards sing the following song at the San Fermín festivities in Pamplona.

Uno de enero,	*January first,*
dos de febrero,	*February second,*
tres de marzo,	*March third,*
cuatro de abril,	*April fourth,*
cinco de mayo,	*May fifth,*
seis de junio,	*June sixth,*
siete de julio,	*July seventh,*
¡San Fermín!	*San Fermín!*

Days of the week

Here is a song involving days of the week that students love to sing.

Lunes, martes, miércoles,	*Monday, Tuesday, Wednesday,*
jueves y viernes,	*Thursday and Friday,*
sábado y domingo,	*Saturday and Sunday,*
sábado y domingo.	*Saturday and Sunday.*
¡No hay clases!	*There are no classes!*
¡No hay clases!	*There are no classes!*

Notice how Ana asks Felipe what day it is today.

ANA   ¿Qué día es hoy?
FELIPE   Hoy es jueves.

Saying the date

When you want to ask today's date, the question is **¿Qué fecha es hoy?**

ANA   ¿Qué fecha es hoy?
FELIPE   Hoy es 15 de agosto de 2002 (quince de agosto de dos mil dos).

To say a date, you need to use numbers. Let's review the numbers so you can be really sure when you say a date.

uno	1	once	11	veintiuno	21
dos	2	doce	12	veintidós	22
tres	3	trece	13	veintitrés	23
cuatro	4	catorce	14	veinticuatro	24
cinco	5	quince	15	veinticinco	25
seis	6	dieciséis	16	veintiséis	26
siete	7	diecisiete	17	veintisiete	27
ocho	8	dieciocho	18	veintiocho	28
nueve	9	diecinueve	19	veintinueve	29
diez	10	veinte	20	treinta	30
				treinta y uno	31

The following poem is probably familiar to you.

Treinta días tiene noviembre	*Thirty days has November*
Con abril, junio y septiembre.	*with April, June, and September.*
El resto tiene treinta y uno	*The rest have 31*
Excepto febrero mocho	*except February,*
Que sólo tiene veinte y ocho.	*which has only 28.*

◄ **2.9** ►
Estructura gramatical

Nouns and definite articles

Nouns and articles must agree in gender and number in Spanish. Usually nouns ending in -**o** are masculine, and those ending in -**a** are feminine. Nouns ending in -**e** and nouns ending in a consonant do not follow a specific rule, so you need to memorize their gender.

el apartamento	*apartment*			
la literatura	*literature*			
el puente	*bridge*	BUT	la fuente	*fountain*
el diente	*tooth*	BUT	la mente	*mind*

There are exceptions to these general rules. For instance, some nouns ending in -**ma** are masculine.

el programa	*program*
el sistema	*system*
el problema	*problem*

And nouns ending in -**ión** or -**d** are feminine!

la canción	*song*
la ciudad	*city*
la universidad	*university*

To make a noun plural, we add an -**s** to singular nouns ending in a vowel (**puente**, **puentes**), or -**es** to singular nouns ending in a consonant (**actor**, **actores**). If the noun ends in -**z**, the plural ending will be -**ces** (**lápiz**, **lápices**). There are four corresponding definite articles.

	SINGULAR	PLURAL
MASCULINE	el	los
FEMININE	la	las

When a plural noun refers to a mixed group, the definite article is **los**. For instance, if there are ten girls in the class but only one boy, we still say **los estudiantes**. You could say that Spanish is a chauvinistic language! Usually a noun ending in -**a** is feminine, while one ending in -**o** is masculine.

el libro	los libros	*book(s)*
la señora	las señoras	*woman (women)*
el esposo y la esposa	los esposos	*husband(s) and wife (wives)*

◄ 2.10 ►
Exercise

¡**Cuál es tu dirección?** Write the following addresses in Spanish.

1. Los Flamingos Ave. #21, Apt. 4B, Quito

2. Sánchez St. #14, Bogotá

_____

3. 183 Muñoz St., Apt. 3D, Caracas

_____

Now, write the following addresses in the correct order.

4. Buenos Aires, Apt. 54, #126 Av. Lavalle

_____

5. #374, Calle Los Limonares, Valparaíso

_____

◄ 2.11 ►
Exercise

Write the question for the following answers.

1. ¿ _____ ?

   Mi número de teléfono es 555-4531.

2. ¿ _____ ?

   Mi dirección es Av. El Bosque No. 35, Quilpué.

3. ¿ _____ ?

   Hoy es jueves.

4. ¿ _____ ?

   Hoy es cuatro de septiembre.

◄ 2.12 ►
Exercise

Complete these sentences with the correct definite articles.

1. _____ lápices son de _____ profesora.

2. _____ señoritas miran _____ tele.

3. _____ profesor y _____ estudiantes son americanos.

4. _____ amigos visitan _____ museo.

5. _____ libro, _____ calculadora y _____ escritorio son nuevos.

6. _____ sábados y _____ domingos no hay clases.

◄ **2.13** ►
Exercise

Write the following dates in Spanish, using words instead of numbers.

1. Thursday, August 5

    _____

2. Monday, July 19

    _____

3. Friday, January 15

    _____

4. Tuesday, October 25

    _____

5. Wednesday, March 11

    _____

 ◄ **2.14** ►
Pitfall

¡Recuerda la concordancia! · *Remember agreement!*

On the recording, listen to the conversation between a female teacher and a student about learning Spanish.

The teacher asks the student if he likes the Spanish class. He is so enthusiastic, that he says that he loves the class and that he loves the teacher. Unfortunately, in his enthusiasm, he makes a mistake: he uses the masculine article **el** with the feminine noun **profesora**. The teacher corrects him in a subtle way, and the student is happy to repeat the correct answer, **la profesora**.

◄ **2.15** ►
Expresión libre

Using what you have learned in this chapter, join in a spontaneous conversation on the recording to review your ability to introduce yourself and give your address and telephone number.

◄ **2.16** ►
¡Viva la diferencia!

• Not only nouns, but also adjectives and articles are either masculine or feminine in Spanish.

• Most nouns ending in **-a** are feminine, and most nouns ending in **-o** are masculine. Of course, there are some exceptions. For instance, the word **artista** is both feminine and masculine, so you can say **el artista** or **la artista** depending on the gender of the artist.

• Telephone numbers are usually spoken in pairs, for example, 4-34, 27-81.

• Months and days are not capitalized in Spanish.

• The Spanish week begins on Monday!

◄ **2.17** ►
How to make it sound Spanish!

In Spanish, we usually stress one word in a sentence.

Me **encanta** la clase.   *I love class.*

When the same vowel is repeated at the end of one word and the beginning of the next word, as in **me encanta**, we do not pronounce both vowels. Only one is pronounced, making it sound like one word.

/**mencanta**/

‹ 3 ›

¡Me encanta este capítulo!
I love this chapter!

OBJECTIVE

In this chapter you will learn the difference between
me encanta ("I love an activity") and **amo** ("I love a
person"), and you will learn to use **-ar** and **-er** verbs
and personal pronouns in statements, questions, and
negative sentences.

◀ 3.1 ▶
DIALOG 1
¡Me encanta _____! · *I love _____!*

David and José are talking about soccer, the most popular sport among Hispanic people. José loves the sport, and David also likes it.

David y José hablan del fútbol, el deporte más popular en Latino-américa. A José le encanta y a David también.

DAVID   José, ¿te gusta el fútbol?
JOSÉ   ¡Me encanta el fútbol!
DAVID   ¡Me gusta el fútbol también, pero amo a mi esposa!
JOSÉ   ¿Qué quieres decir?
DAVID   ¡Los domingos no miramos tele!

◀ 3.2 ▶
Vocabulario

el fútbol	soccer
el deporte	sport
también	also
amo (amar)	I love
¿Qué quieres decir?	What do you mean?
los domingos	on Sundays
no miramos tele	we don't watch TV

Vocabulario adicional

la televisión (tele)	television (TV)
el baloncesto	basketball
el béisbol	baseball
jugar (u>ue)	to play

◀ 3.3 ▶
Comprensión y expresión

In chapter 2 you learned that **me encanta** means "I love." There is a big difference, however, between "I love the Spanish class" (**Me encanta la clase de español**), or even "I love the Spanish teacher" (**Me encanta la profesora de español**), and "I love my wife" (**Amo a mi esposa**) or "I love my parents" (**Amo a mis padres**). While **me encanta** suggests great enthusiasm about the subject, **amo** means that you are in love or that you love a person.

Listen to the recording to practice these examples.

¡Me encanta el tenis!	*I love tennis.*
¡Me encanta la clase de francés!	*I love French class.*
¡Me encanta la profesora de italiano!	*I love the Italian teacher.*
¡Amo a mi mamá!	*I love my mother.*
¡Amo a José!	*I love José.*
¡Amo a mis amigos!	*I love my friends.*

◄ 3.4 ►
Estructura gramatical
Affirmative sentences

Affirmative sentences in Spanish are similar to English sentences: subject + verb + predicate.

Yo soy americano.   *I am American.*

Interrogative sentences

Interrogative sentences in Spanish are different from those in English. While in English you need an auxiliary word ("do," "did," "would," etc.) to begin the sentence, in Spanish you may ask a question by using the same construction as in an affirmative sentence, but raising your voice at the end: **¿Tú eres peruano?** You may also change the position of the verb, placing it at the beginning of the sentence: **¿Eres peruano tú?** In either case, do not forget to raise your voice at the end of the sentence: **¿Eres peruano tú?**

Negative sentences

To form a negative sentence you need to place **no** before the verb.

Ella **no** es profesora.   *She's not a teacher.*

Verbs

The infinitive is the form of the verb you look up in the dictionary. It expresses an action or state without indicating the subject, as in "to eat." When the verb is conjugated, we use personal pronouns to indicate the subject, as in "you eat."

A verb has a stem and an ending. For instance, for the verb **hablar**, the stem is **habl-** and the ending is -ar. While English infinitives begin with "to," Spanish infinitives end in either -**ar**, -**er**, or -**ir**: **hablar** ("to speak"), **comer** ("to eat"), **vivir** ("to live"). These endings are used to designate three general classes of verbs: -**ar**, -**er**, and -**ir**.

In Spanish, the verb endings change to agree with the subject of the verb. For instance, the forms for the first-person singular **yo** ("I") end in -**o** in the present tense. Let's look at the full present tense of a regular -**ar** verb.

HABLAR ("to speak")

yo habl**o**	*I speak*
tú habl**as**	*you (familiar, singular) speak*
él habl**a**	*he speaks*
ella habl**a**	*she speaks*
usted habl**a**	*you (formal, singular) speak*
nosotros habl**amos**	*we speak*
ellos habl**an**	*they (masculine plural) speak*
ellas habl**an**	*they (feminine plural) speak*
ustedes habl**an**	*you (plural) speak*

Notice that three third persons share the same form: the masculine, the feminine, and the formal singular or plural "you." So the verb form for **él**, **ella**, and **usted** is **habla**, and the verb form for **ellos**, **ellas**, and **ustedes** is **hablan**.

Here are some common -**ar** verbs.

trabajar	*to work*
preparar	*to prepare*
cantar	*to sing*
amar	*to love*
comprar	*to buy*
escuchar	*to listen*
mirar	*to watch*
tocar	*to play an instrument*

Personal pronouns

Let's look again at the personal pronouns.

yo	*I*
tú	*you (informal, singular)*
él	*he/it (referring to a masculine noun)*
ella	*she/it (referring to a feminine noun)*
usted*	*you (formal, singular)*
nosotros	*we*
ellos	*they (masculine/mixed group of masculine and feminine)*
ellas	*they (feminine)*
ustedes*	*you (plural)*

An important feature of Spanish is that you do not always need to use these pronouns because, except for the third person, the distinctive ending of the verb indicates the person involved. For instance, you may say either **yo hablo español** or just **hablo español** because the -o ending indicates that the first-person singular "I" is the subject.

ANA	¿Hablas inglés?
FELIPE	Sí, hablo inglés.

When you use the third person, you are more likely to want to use the pronoun (**él**, **ella**, or **Ud.** in the singular; **ellos**, **ellas**, or **Uds.** in the plural) to clarify the subject of the verb.

Yo no hablo, ella habla.   *I don't speak, **she** speaks.*

In this case, it is necessary to emphasize the fact that "she" is the one speaking.

 ◄ **3.5** ►
Audio exercise

On the recording, practice using all forms of the present tense for -**ar** verbs by repeating the following sentences.

Yo miro la tele.	*I am watching television.*
Tú compras un casete.	*You're buying a tape.*

---

*In writing, you can abbreviate **usted** as **Ud.**, and **ustedes** as **Uds.** This is how you will generally see the words written in Spanish text.

Ella ama a sus padres.	*She loves her parents.*
Él prepara arroz con pollo.	*He prepares rice with chicken.*
Usted no escucha la radio.	*You don't listen to the radio.*
Nosotros cantamos "La Cucaracha".	*We sing "La Cucaracha."*
Ellas no trabajan en Madrid.	*They are not working in Madrid.*
Ellos hablan inglés y francés.	*They speak English and French.*
Ustedes miran un programa en español.	*You (all) watch a Spanish-language program.*
Ella toca el violín.	*She plays the violin.*

◄ 3.6 ►
Audio exercise

On the recording you will hear the infinitive form of the verb and the subject. Give the correct form of the verb.

EXAMPLE

PROMPT   hablar (nosotros)
RESPONSE nosotros hablamos

preparar (nosotros)
escuchar (tú)
mirar (Uds.)
comprar (yo)
hablar (Ud.)
trabajar (ella)
escuchar (él)
comprar (ellos)
tocar (nosotros)

◄ 3.7 ►
Audio exercise

Answer the questions on the recording in the affirmative, starting your answer with **Sí** ("Yes").

EXAMPLE

PROMPT   ¿Habla Ud. inglés?   *Do you speak English?*
RESPONSE Sí, yo hablo inglés.   *Yes, I speak English.*

¿Miran Uds. el programa?	*Are you watching the program?*
¿Trabajan ellos en Cádiz?	*Do they work in Cadiz?*
¿Escuchas música clásica?	*Do you listen to classical music?*

¿Compra Eduardo un libro?	*Is Eduardo buying a book?*
¿Canta ópera Plácido Domingo?	*Does Placido Domingo sing opera?*
¿Preparan Uds. un pollo?	*Are you cooking chicken?*

◄ 3.8 ►
Audio exercise

On the recording the speaker will give you three forms of the verb, followed by the rest of the sentence—and then the subject. Complete the sentence with the correct form according to the subject.

EXAMPLE

PROMPT   hablas, hablar, hablamos / inglés—tú

RESPONSE   Tú hablas inglés.

trabajan, trabaja, trabajo / en el Museo del Prado—ella
preparamos, preparo, preparas / arroz con pollo—yo
toco, tocan, tocas / el piano—ellos
canta, cantar, cantamos / muy bien—Caruso
miramos, miro, miran / la tele—Carlos y yo

◄ 3.9 ►
Exercise

Complete the following sentences with the correct form of the verb in parentheses.

1. Nosotros _____ español con el profesor en la clase. (hablar)

2. Ellos _____ en San José, Costa Rica. (trabajar)

3. ¿_____ tú la tele en la tarde? (mirar)

4. Me encanta Alicia de Larrocha. Ella _____ muy bien el piano. (tocar)

5. Uds. no _____ las enchiladas. (preparar)

6. Yo _____ muy mal. (cantar)

7. Alfonso _____ a Berta. (amar)

8. Carolina y Eduardo _____ la radio. (escuchar)

◄ 3.10 ►
Exercise

Complete the following sentences with the correct definite article.

1. _____ cuaderno y _____ libros están en la mesa.

2. _____ profesora y _____ estudiantes hablan español.

3. _____ clase de español es muy interesante.

4. ¿Te gustan _____ fajitas?

5. Me encanta mirar _____ tele.

6. María prepara _____ burritos muy bien.

7. Yo escucho _____ programa deportivo.

8. Ellos visitan _____ monumentos históricos.

◄ 3.11 ►
Exercise

Complete the following sentences with the correct form of the verb in parentheses and the correct definite article.

1. ¿_____ tú _____ lápiz y _____ calculadora? (comprar)

2. _____ profesor y _____ alumnas _____ español. (hablar)

3. Carlos y Josefina _____ _____ piano. (tocar)

4. Margarita _____ _____ burritos. (preparar)

5. _____ helado de chocolate _____ el postre favorito de Elena. (ser)

◄ 3.12 ►
DIALOG 2
¡Me encanta practicar! · *I love to practice!*

David loves Mexican food and he also loves to practice Spanish when he goes to a Mexican restaurant, as on this occasion.

A David le encanta la comida mexicana y también le encanta practicar español.

JOSÉ ¿Te gusta la comida mexicana?

DAVID Me encanta. Anita y yo comemos comida mexicana frecuentemente. Muchas veces como con mis amigos en un restaurante mexicano en la Tercera Avenida. Me encanta practicar español con los meseros.

JOSÉ ¿Comprendes a los meseros cuando hablan rápido?

DAVID Cuando no comprendo, les digo, "No comprendo, repita por favor".

JOSÉ Cuando yo no comprendo, leo el menú.

◄ 3.13 ►
Vocabulario

la comida	*food*
comemos (comer)	*we eat*
frecuentemente	*frequently*
muchas veces	*many times*
tercera	*third*
practicar	*to practice*
los meseros	*waiters*
¿comprendes? (comprender)	*do you understand?*
no comprendo	*I don't understand*
les digo	*I say to them*
repita por favor	*please repeat*
leo (leer)	*I read*
el menú	*menu*

Vocabulario adicional

el plato	*dish*
el arroz con pollo	*rice and chicken*
la comida italiana	*Italian food*
la comida francesa	*French food*
un restaurante español	*a Spanish restaurant*
a veces	*sometimes*
la carta	*menu*

◄ 3.14 ►
Estructura gramatical
Verbs

David says that he and his wife frequently eat Mexican food. He says **comemos**, "we eat," and then **como**, "I eat" in a Mexican restaurant. The verb **comer** ("to eat") is a Spanish **-er** verb. Later in the dialog, David and José use a very important **-er** verb, **comprender** ("to understand"). The endings for **-er** verbs are slightly different from those of **-ar** verbs.

COMER ("to eat")

yo com**o**	*I eat*
tú com**es**	*you (familiar) eat*
él, ella, Ud. com**e**	*he, she eats,*
	you (formal, singular) eat
nosotros com**emos**	*we eat*
ellos, ellas, Uds. com**en**	*they, you (plural) eat*

Here are some common **-er** verbs.

comprender	*to understand*
leer	*to read*
vender	*to sell*
beber	*to drink*
aprender	*to learn*
correr	*to run*

In Spanish, there are three verb types.

1. **regular**: only the ending changes, according to the subject

HABLAR	habl**o**
	habl**as**
	habl**a**
	habl**amos**
	habl**an**

2. **stem-changing**: the ending changes according to the subject, and the stem changes in a pattern

MOVER	m**ue**vo
	m**ue**ves
	m**ue**ve
	mov**emos**
	m**ue**ven

   The stem changes in all forms except **nosotros**.

3. **irregular**: changes occur in the stem and the ending without following a pattern

   We have already seen the irregular verb **ser**.

   > soy
   > eres
   > es
   > somos
   > son

As you can see, every form is different from the infinitive, without following a pattern.

Personal pronouns

Let's review the personal pronouns.

yo	*I*
tú	*you (familiar: for family, children, friends)*
él	*he*
ella	*she*
usted (Ud.)	*you (formal, singular)*
nosotros	*we*
vosotros	*you (plural, used in Spain)*
ellos	*they (masculine)*
ellas	*they (feminine)*
ustedes (Uds.)	*you (plural, used in Latin America)*

As we have seen, personal pronouns are not always used in Spanish because a different verb ending corresponds to each person, for example, **hablo** ("I speak"). However, personal pronouns are used to clarify the third persons that share one singular form and one plural form. For example, the form **habla** on its own could mean "he speaks," "she speaks," or "you speak." Pronouns are also used to emphasize. For example, *Él* **compra el periódico, pero** *yo* **lo leo** emphasizes that "*he* buys the paper, but *I* read it."

Ordinal numbers

David says that he goes to a restaurant on **la Tercera Avenida** ("Third Avenue"). He is using the ordinal **tercera**. Here are the ordinal numbers from 1 to 10.

primero	*first*
segundo	*second*
tercero	*third*
cuarto	*fourth*
quinto	*fifth*
sexto	*sixth*
séptimo	*seventh*
octavo	*eighth*
noveno	*ninth*
décimo	*tenth*

Ordinal numbers agree in gender and number with the noun.

el cuarto piso	*the fourth floor*
la cuarta fila	*the fourth row*
los primeros en llegar	*the first ones to arrive*

Notice that **primero** and **tercero** drop the -o when followed by a masculine noun.

el primer libro *the first book*
BUT el primero *the first one* OR los primeros *the first ones*

el tercer piso *the third floor*
BUT el tercero *the third one* OR los terceros *the third ones*

◄ 3.15 ►
Exercise

Complete the following sentences with the correct ordinal.

1. Me encanta la _____ avenida. (*fifth*)

2. Comemos en la _____ mesa. (*tenth*)

3. Carlos es el _____ estudiante. (*first*)

4. No comprendo la _____ palabra. (*third*)
   (palabra, *word*)

5. No me gustan los _____ platos. (*second*)

◄ **3.16** ►

Audio practice

On the recording, practice **-er** verb forms by repeating the following expressions.

No comprendo.	*I don't understand.*
Ellos aprenden italiano.	*They are learning Italian.*
José come comida mexicana.	*José eats Mexican food.*
¿Bebes agua mineral?	*Are you drinking mineral water?*
No corro en el Parque Central.	*I don't run in Central Park.*
La Sra. Velázquez vende su casa.	*Mrs. Velazquez is selling her house.*
Tú lees y yo aprendo.	*You read and I learn.*

◄ **3.17** ►

Audio exercise

On the recording you will hear the infinitive form of the verb and the subject. Give the correct form of the verb.

EXAMPLE

PROMPT   comer (nosotros)

RESPONSE   comemos

correr (tú)
beber (ellos)
aprender (yo)
comer (Uds.)
leer (ellas)
vender (él)
comprender (nosotros)
aprender (Ud.)

◄ **3.18** ►

Audio exercise

Answer the questions on the recording in the affirmative, starting your answer with **Sí** ("Yes").

EXAMPLE

PROMPT   ¿Comes comida francesa?   *Do you eat French food?*

RESPONSE   Sí, como comida francesa.   *Yes, I eat French food.*

¿Corren Uds. en el parque?	*Do you run in the park?*
¿Beben agua ellos?	*Are they drinking water?*
¿Comprendes el francés?	*Do you understand French?*
¿Lees el periódico?	*Are you reading the newspaper?*
¿Venden ellas la casa?	*Are they selling the house?*
¿Aprende Ud. español?	*Are you learning Spanish?*
¿Comemos en el restaurante mexicano?	*Are we eating in the Mexican restaurant?*

 ◄ **3.19** ►
Audio exercise

On the recording the speaker will give you three forms of an **-er** verb, followed by the rest of the sentence—and then the subject. Complete the sentence with the correct form, according to the subject.

EXAMPLE

PROMPT   Como, comemos, comes / comida mexicana—tú

RESPONSE   Tú comes comida mexicana.

comprendes, comprendemos, comprenden / italiano—nosotros
leen, lees, lee / una revista—ella
bebes, bebo, beben / vino blanco—tú
corremos, corren, corre / en el Parque Central—ellos
vende, vendo, vendemos / un auto—él
aprenden, aprendemos, aprende / a hablar español—Ud.

◄ **3.20** ►
Exercise

Complete the following sentences with the correct form of the verb in parentheses.

1. Ellas _____ una limonada. (beber)

2. Nosotros _____ enchiladas de queso. (comer)

3. Yo _____ bien el francés. (comprender)

4. Ella no _____ una revista española. (leer)

5. ¿_____ tú agua mineral? (beber)

6. Uds. _____ a hablar español. (aprender)

◄ 3.21 ►
Exercise

Complete these sentences with the correct definite article and the correct form of the verb in parentheses.

1. María _____ _____ casa. (vender)

2. Carlos y Rosa _____ muy bien _____ libro. (comprender)

3. Nosotros _____ español en _____ instituto. (aprender)

4. Uds. _____ _____ revista *Time* en inglés. (leer)

5. Yo _____ en _____ restaurante con mis amigos. (comer)

6. Ud. no _____ _____ pregunta. (comprender)

7. Tú _____ café con leche. (beber)

◄ 3.22 ►
Pitfall

¿Amo o me encanta? · *I love* _____?

On the recording, listen to the conversation as a Spanish teacher asks a student whether he likes baseball.

Notice how the student corrects himself. He first uses the verb **amar** instead of saying **me encanta el béisbol**. The verb **amar** is used when we want to say that we love our family, our parents, a lover, and so on. The verb **encantar** is used when we talk about an activity or an object.

◄ 3.23 ►
Expresión libre

Using what you have learned in this chapter, answer the speaker on the recording in a spontaneous conversation about what you like, the languages you can speak, where you work, your profession, and how you learn Spanish.

◄ 3.24 ►
¡Viva la diferencia!

• Spanish-speaking people have developed a second language: they talk with their hands! This amazing language is shared with the French and the Italians. Somehow it seems more meaningful to use your hands to emphasize what you are saying, to the point that in some instances hand gestures take the place of words. For example, to indicate that someone is mean and stingy—without saying it aloud—just touch your elbow. To indicate that someone (it could be you) did something silly or stupid, just touch your forehead with your hand shaped in a fist. And why say "no" when all you need to do is move your index finger in front of the person you are talking to? But be careful: gestures, like some words, may differ from country to country.

◄ 3.25 ►
How to make it sound Spanish

When speaking Spanish, you need to move your mouth much more than when speaking English. You must pronounce the vowels clearly and crisply: **a, e, i, o, u**. These sounds are constant no matter where they appear in the word. Practice saying **mamá, bebé, sí, loco, Lulú**.

Do not forget that you must pronounce every letter (except the initial **h**). When you say the word **leer**, you pronounce the letter **e** two times: **le-er**.

◄ 4 ►

De viaje
On a trip

OBJECTIVE

In this chapter you will learn how to say "it is necessary" to do something, or "one must _____"; how
to use demonstratives and indefinite articles; and **-ir**
verbs and vocabulary related to travel.

◄ **4.1** ►

DIALOG 1
Haciendo las maletas · *Packing*

David and his wife, Anita, are packing. The day of their trip to Mexico has arrived, and they are getting ready. They help each other remember to take some very important things, such as the camera and the address book.

David y Anita hacen las maletas. Anita pregunta si necesitan abrir las maletas en el aeropuerto y si David tiene su libreta de direcciones. David lleva la cámara porque a Anita le encanta tomar fotos.

ANITA ¿Hay que abrir las maletas en el aeropuerto?

DAVID Creo que solamente es necesario abrir el equipaje de mano.

ANITA ¿Tienes tu libreta de direcciones? Tú siempre escribes tarjetas postales a tus amigos.

DAVID Sí, tengo mi libreta de direcciones. También tengo nuestra cámara. Te encanta tomar fotos, ¿verdad?

ANITA Sí, me encanta tomar fotos. Gracias por recordar la cámara.

◄ **4.2** ►
Vocabulario

hacen las maletas	*they are packing*
pregunta (preguntar)	*she asks (a question)*
si	*if*
abrir	*to open*
las maletas	*suitcases*
tiene (tener) (*irregular*)	*he has*
la libreta de direcciones	*address book*
lleva (llevar)	*he carries, takes along*
la cámara	*camera*
porque	*because*
tomar fotos	*to take pictures*
el equipaje de mano	*hand luggage*
escribes (escribir)	*you write*
las tarjetas postales	*postcards*
recordar (o>ue)	*to remember*

Vocabulario adicional

revisar	*to check*
las cartas	*letters*
los sellos	*stamps*
el rollo de película	*roll of film*
olvidar	*to forget*

Expresión idiomática

Although there is a verb meaning to pack (**empacar**), the most common way to say this in Spanish is **hacer la maleta** or **hacer las maletas**.

 ◄ **4.3** ►
Comprensión y expresión

Must we?

When we want to ask if we must do something, we ask **¿Hay que?** followed by an infinitive. We can also convey this idea by saying that it is necessary to do something, **Es necesario** _____, followed by an infinitive. Anita asked David if they must open the suitcases (**¿Hay que abrir las maletas?**) at the airport, and he answered that **es necesario abrir** only the hand luggage. Look at the following examples.

¿Hay que abrir la puerta?	*Must one open the door?*
¿Hay que escribir una carta?	*Must one write a letter?*
¿Hay que vivir en la ciudad?	*Must one live in the city?*
¿Es necesario permitir eso?	*Is it necessary to allow that?*
¿Es necesario cubrir el libro?	*Is it necessary to cover the book?*

Is that so?

David tells Anita, **Te encanta tomar fotos, ¿verdad?** To say "right?," "isn't it?," or "doesn't it?" you simply add **¿verdad?** after the statement. Look at the following examples.

Tienes la cámara, ¿verdad?	*You have the camera, right?*
Escribes una tarjeta postal, ¿verdad?	*You're writing a postcard, aren't you?*
Ella toma fotos, ¿verdad?	*She's taking photos, isn't she?*
No te gusta hacer las maletas, ¿verdad?	*You don't like to do the packing, do you?*
Hay que preguntar, ¿verdad?	*We have to ask, right?*

◄ 4.4 ►

Audio exercise

Listen to the recording and answer the questions. Based on the prompt, answer in the negative or the affirmative.

EXAMPLE

PROMPT   ¿Hay que tomar fotos de la ciudad? /
          (*No, we have many photos.*)
RESPONSE No, no hay que tomar fotos de la ciudad.

¿Hay que abrir la puerta? / (*It is very warm in here.*)
¿Hay que escribir una carta? / (*We want to complain.*)
¿Hay que preparar el equipaje? / (*Yes, it is getting late.*)
¿Es necesario comer en un restaurante? / (*I don't think so.*)
¿Es necesario leer el periódico? / (*Yes, I think so.*)

◄ 4.5 ►

Estructura gramatical

We have studied **-ar** and **-er** verbs. Now we turn to the third conjugation, **-ir** verbs, which are not too different from **-er** verbs. Actually, only the first-person plural ("we") form is different, **-imos**. Let's use the verb **vivir** ("to live") as the model verb. All other regular **-ir** verbs follow the same pattern.

VIVIR ("to live")

yo viv**o**	*I live*
tú viv**es**	*you (familiar) live*
él, ella, Ud. viv**e**	*he, she lives, you (formal, singular) live*
nosotros viv**imos**	*we live*
ellos, ellas, Uds. viv**en**	*they, you (plural) live*

Here are some common **-ir** verbs.

vivir	*to live*
abrir	*to open*
permitir	*to allow*
escribir	*to write*
decidir	*to decide*
recibir	*to receive*

◄ 4.6 ►
Audio practice

On the recording, practice **-ir** verbs in the present tense by repeating the following sentences.

Yo abro la puerta.	*I open the door.*
Tú decides hacer las maletas.	*You decide to do the packing.*
Ella no permite fumar.	*She does not allow smoking.*
Jorge escribe tarjetas postales.	*Jorge is writing postcards.*
Nosotros vivimos en la ciudad.	*We live in the city.*
Ellos reciben una carta.	*They receive a letter.*
Uds. abren las maletas.	*You are opening the baggage.*

◄ 4.7 ►
Audio exercise

On the recording you will hear the infinitive form of the verb and the subject. Give the correct form of the verb.

EXAMPLE

PROMPT	abrir (mis amigos)
RESPONSE	mis amigos abren

vivir (nosotros)	recibir (yo)
permitir (Ud.)	abrir (la señora Molina)
decidir (ellos)	escribir (los profesores)

◄ 4.8 ►
Audio exercise

Answer the questions on the recording in the affirmative, starting your answer with **Sí**.

EXAMPLE

PROMPT	¿Abre Ud. la ventana?	*Are you opening the window?*
RESPONSE	Sí, yo abro la ventana.	*Yes, I'm opening the window.*

¿Decides preparar el equipaje?	*Are you deciding to pack the luggage?*
¿Escribe Juan una tarjeta postal?	*Is Juan writing a postcard?*
¿Decides ir al teatro?	*Are you deciding to go to the theater?*
¿Permitimos abrir la ventana?	*Do we allow the window to be opened?*

¿Viven tus amigos en una casa?	*Do your friends live in a house?*
¿Recibe Ud. muchas cartas?	*Do you receive many letters?*

◄ 4.9 ►
Audio exercise

On the recording the speaker will give you three forms of an -**ir** verb, followed by the rest of the sentence—and then the subject. Complete the sentence with the correct verb form according to the subject.

EXAMPLE

PROMPT   viven, vives, vivimos / en una casa grande—ustedes
RESPONSE   Uds. viven en una casa grande.

permito, permitimos, permite / abrir la puerta—nosotros
viven, vive, vivo / en el campo—ella
recibo, recibes, recibe / una tarjeta postal—yo
decides, decidimos, deciden / ir al teatro—ellos
escribimos, escribes, escribe / una novela—tú
abrimos, abres, abre / la ventana—nosotros

◄ 4.10 ►
DIALOG 2
En el aeropuerto · *At the airport*

David and his wife, Anita, are at the airport on their way to Mexico. Although they are at Kennedy Airport in New York, they speak Spanish at the counter because they don't want to miss any opportunities!

David y Anita bajan del taxi, entran en el terminal de Aeroméxico y van al mostrador de la aerolínea.

DAVID	Buenas tardes, señorita. ¿Habla Ud. español?
AGENTE	Sí, hablo español. Muy buenas tardes. ¿Son Uds. mexicanos?
ANITA	No, somos americanos, pero queremos practicar español.
AGENTE	¡Ah! ¡Muy bien! Los pasajes y sus pasaportes, por favor. ¿Cuántas maletas tienen?
DAVID	Estas dos maletas.
AGENTE	¿Equipaje de mano?
ANITA	Tengo este bolso solamente.
DAVID	Yo tengo una computadora y unos papeles en este maletín.
AGENTE	Bien. Aquí tienen las tarjetas de embarque. Favor de embarcar por la puerta de salida 4A. ¡Buen viaje!

◄ **4.11** ►
Vocabulario

bajan de	*they get out of, get off, go down*
entran en	*they enter*
el terminal	*terminal*
van al mostrador de la aerolínea	*they go to the airline counter*
queremos practicar	*we want to practice*
los pasajes	*tickets*
¿cuántas?	*how many?*
las maletas	*suitcases*
tienen (tener) (*irregular*)	*you have*
tengo (tener) (*irregular*)	*I have*
el bolso	*bag*
la computadora	*computer*
este maletín	*this briefcase*
aquí tienen	*here you have*
la tarjeta de embarque	*boarding pass*
favor de embarcar	*please board (the airplane)*
por la puerta de salida	*through the departure gate*
¡Buen viaje!	*Have a good trip!*

Vocabulario adicional

el avión	*airplane*
el asiento	*seat*
la ventanilla	*small window*
el centro	*center*
el pasillo	*aisle*
un vuelo directo	*a direct flight*
hacer escala en	*to make a stopover*
el pasaje de ida y vuelta	*round-trip ticket*
facturar el equipaje	*to check the luggage*
reclamar el equipaje	*to claim the luggage*
el/la auxiliar de vuelo	*flight assistant*
abrocharse el cinturón de seguridad	*to fasten the seat belt*
la llegada	*arrival*
la salida	*departure*
el pasajero/la pasajera	*passenger*

◄ 4.12 ►
Estructura gramatical
Demonstrative adjectives

When we want to say "this" or "those," we use demonstratives.

este, esta	*this (masculine/feminine)*
estos, estas	*these (masculine/feminine)*
ese, esa	*that*
esos, esas	*those*
aquel, aquella	*that (over there, far away)*
aquellos, aquellas	*those (over there, far away)*

So you will say **Prefiero** *este* **vuelo, pero ella prefiere** *esa* **aerolínea** ("I prefer *this* flight, but she prefers *that* airline").

Notice that a demonstrative has an accent when there is no noun: **Prefiero** *esa* **aerolínea**, but **Prefiero** *ésa*.

Listen to the recording to practice the following examples.

este pasaje	*this ticket*
esta puerta	*this door*
estos aviones	*these airplanes*
estas ventanas	*these windows*
ese pasaje de ida y vuelta	*that round-trip ticket*
esa auxiliar de vuelo	*that flight attendant*
esos cinturones de seguridad	*those seat belts*
esas puertas de salida	*those departure gates*
aquel avión	*that airplane over there*
aquella maleta	*that suitcase over there*
aquellos asientos	*those seats over there*
aquellas tarjetas de embarque	*those boarding passes*

Definite articles

David tells the agent at the airport that he has **una computadora y unos papeles**, that is, "a computer and some papers." The indefinite articles are **un, una, unos, unas**. Indefinite articles, as well as definite articles, must agree in gender and number with the noun they modify. This is why there are four indefinite articles: singular masculine and feminine, and plural masculine and feminine. Let's practice using these articles. Look at the following examples.

un avión	*an airplane*
una auxiliar de vuelo	*a flight attendant*
unos asientos en el centro	*some center seats*
unas aerolíneas	*some airlines*

 ◄ **4.13** ►
Audio practice

How do we say "this, these, that, those"? Let's practice the demonstratives. On the recording, listen to David talking to the agent and repeat what they say.

AGENTE   ¿Esa maleta es su equipaje?

DAVID   No, estas maletas son mi equipaje.

AGENTE   ¿Este pasaje es su pasaje?

DAVID   No, ese pasaje es mi pasaje.

AGENTE   ¿Aquella señora es su esposa?

DAVID   ¡Sí! ¡Aquella señora es mi esposa!

◄ **4.14** ►
Exercise

Complete the following phrases with the correct demonstrative.

EXAMPLE   *esa* aerolínea (*that*)

1. _____ computadoras (*these*)

2. _____ cinturón de seguridad (*this*)

3. _____ asientos (*those over there*)

4. _____ pasaje (*that*)

5. _____ ventana (*that over there*)

6. _____ puerta de salida (*that*)

◄ **4.15** ►
Exercise

Complete the following phrases with the correct indefinite article.

EXAMPLE   *un* asiento junto a la ventanilla

1. _____ maleta

2. _____ tarjetas de embarque

3. _____ cinturón de seguridad

4. _____ pasaje de ida y vuelta

5. _____ aeropuerto

6. _____ aviones

◄ 4.16 ►
Pitfall

Los demostrativos · *Demonstratives*

On the recording, listen to a conversation as the teacher is reviewing the demonstratives and the indefinite articles with a student who has some difficulties.

The student probably thought that the plural of **este** is **estes**. Careful! The masculine plural is **estos**! Also, remember that the objects that are *here* are **estos objetos**; the objects that are *there* are **esos objetos**; and the objects that are *over there* are **aquellos objetos**.

◄ 4.17 ►
Exercise

Review the demonstratives again by connecting the Spanish phrase to its English equivalent.

ese	profesores	*this window*
estas	equipaje	1. *these doors*
esos	ventana	2. *this stamp*
aquella	pasajes	3. *these seats*
esta	cartas	4. *that lady*
aquellos	sello	5. *those letters*
este	señora	6. *that airport*
esas	tarjetas	7. *those tickets*
aquel	puertas	8. *that (female) teacher over there*
esa	asientos	9. *that luggage over there*
aquellas	profesora	10. *those cards over there*
estos	aeropuerto	11. *those teachers over there*

◄ 4.18 ►
Audio practice

Give the correct indefinite article that corresponds to the noun you hear on the recording.

EXAMPLE

PROMPT	sellos	*stamps*
RESPONSE	unos sellos	*some stamps*

puerta	*door*
aerolínea	*airline*
asiento	*seat*
pasaje	*ticket*
pasajeros	*passengers*

◄ 4.19 ►
Expresión libre

Using what you have learned in this chapter, practice -**ir** verb forms and definite articles by answering the speaker on the recording in a spontaneous conversation.

◄ 4.20 ►
¡Viva la diferencia!

• In Spanish there are four personal pronouns meaning "you"! If you want to address one person, you have two choices. **Ud.** (**usted**) is the way to address people you don't know well, or to show respect. **Tú**, the informal form, is used to address family, children, friends, fellow students, and work colleagues.

If you want to address a group of people, you also have two choices. These pronouns, however, are not formal or informal, but regional. In Latin America they use **Uds.** (**ustedes**) to address a group of friends or unknown people; in Spain, they use **vosotros**. So when you are in Spain you will hear **vosotros**, which takes a different verb ending (**vosotros habláis, vosotros coméis, vosotros vivís**), but when in Latin America you will hear **ustedes**.

Although the proper use of **tú** and **Ud.** is very important in Spain, South America, and Central America, it is less important in the Caribbean countries (Cuba, Dominican Republic, and Puerto Rico), where **tú** is widely used. As a matter of fact, young people increasingly use only the pronoun **tú** everywhere. The word in Spanish that means to address someone informally is **tutear** ("to address with the **tú** form").

◄ **4.21** ►
How to make it sound Spanish

How do we pronounce Spanish consonants?

The consonants **b** and **v** are pronounced very much alike.

burro	*donkey*
invierno	*winter*

In Latin America, **c** is pronounced /s/ when followed by **e** or **i**, but /k/ when followed by **a**, **o**, or **u**.

cesta	/sesta/	casa	/kasa/
cine	/sine/	cosa	/kosa/
		cuna	/kuna/

In Spain, **c** followed by **e** or **i** is pronounced "th" as in English "think."

cesta	/thesta/
cine	/thine/

The consonant **d** is usually pronounced /d/ as in English "dame." However, when **d** is in the endings **-ado**, **-ada**, **-edo**, **-eda**, etc., the pronunciation is "th" as in English "mother."

donde	/donde/	cada	/catha/
		dedo	/detho/

The consonants **f**, **m**, and **n** are pronounced the same as in English.

◄ 5 ►

Llegando al hotel
Arriving at the hotel

OBJECTIVE

In this chapter you will learn the possessive adjectives; the verb **tener** ("to have") and several common expressions that use this verb; how to tell the actual time and ask at what time something takes place; how to ask "Do you want to _____" or "How can I help you?"; how to answer "I want to _____" or "I would like to _____"; and, very important, how to say "Thank you" and "You are welcome." When you finish this chapter you should feel comfortable using the new vocabulary related to taking a taxi ride and registering at a hotel.

◄ 5.1 ►
DIALOG 1
En un taxi · *In a taxi*

David and Anita have arrived in Mexico City. When they take a taxi to the hotel, they have to give the hotel address. Anita wants to know what time it is, because Mexico City is in a different time zone. Half an hour later they arrive at the hotel. David asks how much the ride is, and Anita sounds relieved that it is only 90 pesos.

David y su esposa Anita toman un taxi del aeropuerto Benito Juárez al hotel en México D.F.

TAXISTA	Buenas tardes, señores. ¿Adónde quieren ir?
ANITA	Queremos ir al hotel Hernán Cortés.
TAXISTA	¿La dirección del hotel, por favor?
DAVID	Avenida Juárez N° 43.
ANITA	Señorita, ¿qué hora es?
TAXISTA	Son las cuatro de la tarde, señora.
ANITA	¡Gracias!
TAXISTA	De nada.

(media hora más tarde)

TAXISTA	El hotel Hernán Cortés, señores.
DAVID	¿Cuánto es?
TAXISTA	Son $90.
ANITA	¡Muchas gracias!

◄ 5.2 ►
Vocabulario

toman un taxi	*they take a taxi*
¿Adónde quieren ir?	*Where do you want to go?*
queremos ir	*we want to go*
al hotel	*to the hotel*
por favor	*please*
¿Qué hora es?	*What time is it?*
Son las cuatro de la tarde.	*It is four in the afternoon.*
media hora	*half an hour*
más tarde	*later*
¿Cuánto es?	*How much is it?*

◄ **5.3** ►

Comprensión y expresión

Do you want to?

When we want to ask "Do you want to _____," we say **¿Quieres** _____ (informal), **¿Quiere** _____ (formal), or **¿Quieren** _____ (plural), followed by an infinitive. The answer in the singular is **quiero**, and in the plural **queremos**.

SINGULAR

INFORMAL	**¿Quieres** ir al aeropuerto? ⎱	*Do you want to go*
FORMAL	**¿Quiere** ir al aeropuerto? ⎰	*to the airport?*
	No, **quiero** ir al hotel.	*No, I want to go to the hotel.*

You may also answer with the more polite form **quisiera**, meaning "I would like _____."

¿Quieres tomar un refresco? ⎱ **¿Quiere** tomar un refresco? ⎰	*Do you want a cold drink?*
Sí, **quisiera** tomar una limonada.	*Yes, I would like a lemonade.*

PLURAL

¿Quieren ir al aeropuerto?	*Do you want to go to the airport?*
Sí, **queremos** ir al aeropuerto.	*Yes, we want to go to the airport.*

You may also use the more polite form.

¿Quieren comer algo?	*Would you like to eat something?*
Sí, **quisiéramos** comer un sandwich.	*Yes, we would like to eat a sandwich.*

Saying the time

When the question is **¿Qué hora es?** ("What time is it?"), the answer is always **Son las** _____, unless it is around 1 o'clock. Then the answer is **Es la una.**

¿Qué hora es?

Es la una de la tarde.

(*You must use* es *because* una *is singular.*)

Son las 9:30 de la noche.

(*For 9:30 say* nueve y treinta OR nueve y media.)

Son las 12 del día. OR Es el mediodía.

Son las 2:15 de la madrugada.

(*For 2:15 say* dos y quince OR dos y cuarto.)

1:25 A.M.	Es la una y veinticinco de la madrugada.
3:45 A.M.	Son las tres y cuarenta y cinco de la madrugada.
	OR Son las cuatro menos quince.
	OR Son las cuatro menos cuarto.
	(*It is not 4 A.M. yet; in fact, we still have 15 minutes to go.*)
9:15 A.M.	Son las nueve y cuarto (quince) de la mañana.
12 noon	Son las doce del día. OR Es el mediodía.
3:30 P.M.	Son las tres y media (treinta) de la tarde.
4:55 P.M.	Son las cuatro y cincuenta y cinco (Son las cinco menos cinco) de la tarde.
12 midnight	Son las doce de la noche.
	OR Es la medianoche.

Notice that you say **de la noche**, but **del día. Del** is a contraction formed with **de** and **el**. There are only two contractions in Spanish: **al** (**a** + **el**) and **del** (**de** + **el**). Unlike English, there is no alternative; you must use the contraction.

Saying thank you

If you are extremely thankful, you may say **¡Muchas gracias!** or even **¡Muchísimas gracias!** The response to such thanks is always **De nada** or **No hay de qué**.

Asking how much it costs

When we need to know how much we need to pay for something, we say **¿Cuánto es?**

SITUATION   Cecilia picks up an orange at the fruit stand.

CECILIA   ¿Cuánto es?
VENDEDOR   Es un peso.

SITUATION   David asks for two tickets at the subway booth.

DAVID   ¿Cuánto es?
VENDEDOR   Son cinco pesos.

◄ 5.4 ►
Audio practice

We heard the taxi driver ask David where they wanted to go, to which David answered that they wanted to go to the hotel. Let's practice how to ask whether someone wants to do something and how to answer in a direct way by saying **quiero**, or in a more polite way by saying **quisiera**. Look at the following conversations.

ANITA   David, ¿quieres ir al hotel?

DAVID   No, quiero ir al Museo de Antropología. ¿Y tú?

ANITA   Quisiera ir a la casa de Frida Kahlo.

Catalina, her little son Linito, and her friend Anita are at a restaurant. The waiter is waiting for their order.

CATALINA   Anita, ¿quieres tomar una bebida?

ANITA   Quisiera tomar una limonada.

CATALINA   Linito, ¿qué quieres tomar?

LINITO   ¡Quiero agua!

CATALINA   Por favor, dos limonadas y ¡agua!

◄ 5.5 ►
Exercise

Complete the following questions and answers with the correct word: **quiero, quieres, quiere, queremos,** or **quieren.**

1. DAVID   ¿Qué _____ tomar, Anita?

2. ANITA   _____ tomar agua.

3. DAVID   ¿Qué _____ tomar, Carlos y Raquel?

4. RAQUEL   _____ tomar agua también. (también, *also*)

5. DAVID   ¿Qué _____ comer, Carlos y Raquel?

6. CARLOS Y RAQUEL _____ comer arroz con pollo. ¿Y tú?

7. DAVID   _____ comer chile con carne.

8. CARLOS   ¿Qué _____ comer, Anita?

9. ANITA   _____ comer arroz con pollo
también.

◄ 5.6 ►
Exercise

Do you remember how Anita asked the driver the time? She asked **¿Qué hora es?** and he answered **Son las cuatro.** Let's practice how to ask and tell time. Look at the following conversations.

DAVID	Anita, ¿qué hora es?
ANITA	Son las dos y treinta de la tarde.
EDUARDO	No, ¡son las dos y treinta y cinco!
DAVID	¡Muchas gracias!
EDUARDO	¡De nada!

Now here is María talking to Pablo.

MARÍA	¿Qué hora es?
PABLO	¡Es la una de la madrugada!
MARÍA	¡Es muy tarde! ¡Adiós!

Listen to the recording and write the times (in numerical form) that you hear. **¿Qué hora es?**

1. _____

2. _____

3. _____

4. _____

5. _____

6. _____

◄ 5.7 ►
Exercise

¿Qué hora es? Write the times shown on the clocks below, using words, not figures.

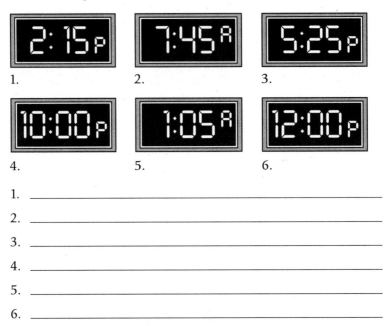

1.   2.   3.

4.   5.   6.

1. _____

2. _____

3. _____

4. _____

5. _____

6. _____

 ### ◄ 5.8 ►
DIALOG 2
En el hotel · *At the hotel*

David and Anita have arrived at the hotel. They go to the reception desk and talk to the receptionist.

David y Anita llegan al hotel Hernán Cortés y hablan con la recepcionista.

RECEPCIONISTA	¿En qué puedo servirles?
DAVID	Tenemos una reservación para hoy y mañana, a nombre de David y Anita Wood.
RECEPCIONISTA	Sí, aquí tengo su reservación para una habitación con baño privado para dos personas.
DAVID	¿Cuánto es la habitación?
RECEPCIONISTA	Son 850 pesos por noche, con desayuno.

DAVID	Muy bien. Aquí está mi tarjeta de crédito. ¿A qué hora es el desayuno?
RECEPCIONISTA	El desayuno es desde las siete hasta las diez de la mañana, en el comedor.
DAVID	Gracias.
RECEPCIONISTA	De nada, señor.
ANITA	Por favor, ¿cuál es el número de nuestra habitación?
RECEPCIONISTA	El número de su habitación es 452.
ANITA	¿A qué hora debemos desocupar la habitación el día de la partida?
RECEPCIONISTA	Deben desocupar la habitación a las doce del día. ¡Bienvenidos a México!

(El botones toma las maletas y camina al ascensor.)

◄ 5.9 ►
Vocabulario

llegan (llegar)	*they arrive*
el/la recepcionista	*receptionist*
¿En qué puedo servirle(s)?	*How may I help you?*
tenemos (tener) (*irregular*)	*we have*
aquí	*here*
la habitación	*room*
el baño privado	*private bathroom*
con desayuno	*with breakfast*
la tarjeta de crédito	*credit card*
el comedor	*dining room*
¿cuál es el número de _____?	*what is the number of _____?*
debemos (deber)	*we must*
el día de la partida	*day of departure*
desocupar	*to vacate*
bienvenidos a _____	*welcome to _____*
el botones	*bellboy*
toma (tomar)	*he takes*
camina (caminar)	*he walks*
el ascensor	*elevator*

◄ **5.10** ►

Estructura gramatical

Possessives

In the dialog David mentions **mi tarjeta de crédito** ("my credit card") and **nuestra habitación** ("our room"), and the manager says **su habitación**, meaning "your room." Let's look at the possessive adjectives in Spanish.

mi(s)	*my*	mi amigo, mis amigos
tu(s)	*your*	tu habitación, tus habitaciones
su(s)	*his, her, your (for Ud. or Uds.), their*	su hotel, sus maletas
nuestro(-a)(s)	*our*	nuestra maleta, nuestro baño, nuestras maletas, nuestros baños

In Spanish, possessives agree in gender with the noun they modify. So "their house" is **su casa**.

The verb **tener**

When David says **tenemos una reservación** ("we have a reservation"), the manager says, **Sí, aquí tengo su reservación** ("Yes, I have your reservation here"). The verb "to have" is **tener** in Spanish, and it is an irregular verb.

tengo	Tengo una reservación. *I have a reservation.*
tienes	¿Tienes tu tarjeta de crédito? *Do you have your credit card?*
tiene	La señora no tiene su pasaporte. *The lady does not have her passport.*
tenemos	Tenemos dos maletas. *We have two pieces of luggage.*
tienen	Las señoras tienen el número 24. *The ladies have number 24.*

The verb **tener** means "to have," but it is also used in many expressions.

tener frío	*to be cold*
tener calor	*to be warm*
tener hambre	*to be hungry*
tener sed	*to be thirsty*
tener sueño	*to be sleepy*
tener miedo	*to be afraid*
tener razón	*to be right*
tener ganas de	*to feel like*
tener _____ años	*to be _____ years old*

◄ **5.11** ►
Comprensión y expresión

When we want to know at what time something takes place, we ask **¿A qué hora es** _____**?**

¿A qué hora es el almuerzo?	*What time is lunch?*
El almuerzo es a las dos de la tarde.	*Lunch is at two in the afternoon.*

When we want to help someone, we ask **¿En qué puedo servirlo/servirla?**

¿En qué puedo servirla, señora?	*May I help you, ma'am?*
Quisiera hacer una reservación...	*I would like to make a reservation . . .*
¿Para cuándo (qué fecha)?	*For when (what date)?*
Para el lunes 27 de agosto.	*For Monday, August 27.*

◄ **5.12** ►
Audio practice

Tener ("to have") is one of the verbs most used in Spanish. Here are its forms.

tengo
tienes
tiene
tenemos
tienen

In the following conversation, David is talking to the hotel manager. Anita then asks David whether he has her passport. What a relief, he has it! It is easy to lose a passport.

ENCARGADA	¿Tienen Uds. una reservación?
DAVID	Sí, tenemos una reservación.
ENCARGADA	¿Tienen Uds. sus pasaportes?
DAVID	Sí, tengo mi pasaporte.
ANITA	David, ¿no tienes mi pasaporte?
DAVID	Un momento. Sí, aquí tengo tu pasaporte.
ANITA	¡Uf!

 ◄ **5.13** ►
Audio exercise

Complete the exercise on the recording, then answer the questions below, using the correct form of **tener**.

1. ¿Tiene Ud. su pasaje?

   Sí, _____ mi pasaje.

2. ¿Tienes tú la maleta?

   No, yo no _____ la maleta.

3. ¿Tiene ella mi pasaje?

   Sí, ella _____ su pasaje.

4. ¿Tienen Uds. nuestro número?

   No, nosotros no _____ su número.

5. ¿Tienen ellas la habitación 203?

   No, ellas _____ la 204.

 ◄ **5.14** ►
Audio practice

There are several expressions that use **tener**. For instance, **tener frío** is "to be cold." Here is what Anita and David say late one afternoon, after walking through México City.

ANITA	¿Tienes frío?
DAVID	No, tengo calor. ¡Estamos en julio!

ANITA   Tienes razón. ¿Tienes sed?

DAVID   Sí, tengo mucha sed. Quisiera tomar algo. (algo, *something*)

ANITA   Pues yo tengo hambre. ¿Tienes ganas de comer?

DAVID   Sí, tengo ganas de comer también. Vamos a ese café.

When Anita tells David **tienes razón**, she is saying that he is right, it is hot in July. Did you recognize **tener sed** and **tener hambre**? Did you notice that David did not say **¿Quieres comer?** ("Do you want to eat?"), but **¿Tienes ganas de comer?** ("Do you feel like eating?")?

◀ 5.15 ▶
Exercise

Complete the following sentences with an appropriate form of **tener hambre, tener frío**, etc.

1. Cuando _____, tomo agua.

2. Cuando _____, comemos algo.

3. En julio nosotros _____.

4. En enero tú _____.

5. ¿Cuántos años _____ tú? —_____ 20 años.

6. Cuando _____, grito. (gritar, *to scream*)

7. Tú siempre _____ razón.

◀ 5.16 ▶
Audio practice

On the recording, listen to how Mr. López asks the owner of a **pensión** the time of each meal.

SR. LÓPEZ   ¿A qué hora es el desayuno?

DUEÑO   El desayuno es a las siete de la mañana.

SR. LÓPEZ   ¿A qué hora es el almuerzo?

DUEÑO   El almuerzo es a la una de la tarde.

SR. LÓPEZ   ¿A qué hora es la cena?

DUEÑO   La cena es a las ocho de la noche.

◄ **5.17** ►
Audio practice

Let's practice asking and telling what time it is, and also at what time an event takes place. Anita is talking to David while she is taking a shower. As you can hear on the recording, she is having problems hearing the right answer.

ANITA   ¿Qué hora es?
DAVID   Son las 5:15 de la tarde.
ANITA   ¿Son las 6:15?
DAVID   No, son las 5:15.
ANITA   ¿A qué hora es la cena?
DAVID   La cena es a las ocho de la noche.
ANITA   ¿A qué hora?
DAVID   ¡A las ocho!

◄ **5.18** ►
Exercise

Answer the following questions in complete sentences.

EXAMPLE   ¿Qué hora es? (5 P.M.)
   <u>Son las cinco de la tarde.</u>

1. ¿Qué hora es? (9:20 P.M.)

_____

2. ¿Qué hora es? (12 midnight)

_____

3. ¿Qué hora es? (2:50 P.M.)

_____

4. ¿A qué hora es el desayuno? (7:30 A.M.)

_____

5. ¿A qué hora es la cena? (8 P.M.)

_____

6. ¿A qué hora es el almuerzo? (1 P.M.)

_____

 ◄ **5.19** ►

DIALOG 3
Quisiera hacer una reservación · *I would like to make a reservation*

Now Anita makes a reservation at a hotel in Acapulco.

Anita quiere hacer una reservación en el Hotel Carreño para el 14 de julio. Ella quiere una habitación doble con baño privado.

ANITA	¿Aló?
ENCARGADA	¡Aló! Hotel Carreño. ¿En qué puedo servirla?
ANITA	Quisiera hacer una reservación.
ENCARGADA	¿Para qué fecha?
ANITA	Para el próximo viernes, 14 de julio, hasta el domingo, 16 de julio.
ENCARGADA	Un momento, por favor. Durante el verano generalmente el hotel está completo. ¿Para cuántas personas?
ANITA	Para dos personas. Quisiera una habitación con baño privado.
ENCARGADA	Tiene suerte, tenemos una habitación doble con baño privado desde el 14 hasta el 16 de julio.
ANITA	¿Cuánto es la habitación?
ENCARGADA	Una habitación doble con desayuno es 688 pesos, más el IVA y el impuesto de hospedaje. Es un total de 805 pesos.
ANITA	Muchas gracias.

◄ **5.20** ►
Vocabulario

el encargado/la encargada	*manager*
¿Para qué fecha?	*For what date?*
para el próximo viernes	*for next Friday*
un momento, por favor	*one moment, please*
durante el verano	*during the summer*
el hotel está completo	*the hotel is full*
desde _____ hasta	*from _____ until*
más	*plus*
IVA	*value-added tax, VAT*
el impuesto de hospedaje	*lodging tax*
un total de	*a total of*

Vocabulario adicional

las estaciones	*the seasons*
el verano	*summer*
el otoño	*fall*
el invierno	*winter*
la primavera	*spring*
estamos completos	*we are booked up*

◄ 5.21 ►
Audio exercise

Do you think you can use the possessives now? Remember that the singular possessives are **mi**, **tu**, **su**, **nuestro**, **su**. The plural forms, **mis**, **tus**, **sus**, are used with plural nouns. **Nuestro** and **nuestros** have feminine forms: **nuestra** (used with feminine singular nouns) and **nuestras** (used with feminine plural nouns). Answer the following questions in the affirmative.

EXAMPLE

PROMPT   ¿Tienes mi pasaporte?
RESPONSE   Sí, tengo tu pasaporte.

¿Son tus maletas?	*Are these your suitcases?*
¿Es tu reservación?	*Is this your reservation?*
¿Son nuestras habitaciones?	*Are these our rooms?*
¿Tienen Uds. mi maleta?	*Do you have my suitcase?*
¿Es nuestro desayuno?	*Is this our breakfast?*

◄ 5.22 ►
Expresión libre

Answer the speaker on the recording in a spontaneous conversation. First, imagine that you are a manager at a hotel. A gentleman comes to register. What would you tell him? Then, imagine you are calling to make a reservation at a hotel.

◄ 5.23 ►
¡Viva la diferencia!

• In Spanish-speaking countries, many hotels offer a rate that includes breakfast. Instead of going to a hotel or motel, a more reasonable accommodation is the **pensión**, where meals are also offered. It is possible to pay a rate called **media pensión**, which includes breakfast and either lunch or dinner, or to pay a little more for a **pensión completa**, which includes a room and three meals. This type of accommodation is favored by students and people who need room and board for an extended period of time.

• Mexico has a value-added tax of 15% called IVA (**impuesto de valor agregado**), as well as a lodging tax of 2%.

◄ **5.24** ►
How to make it sound Spanish

The consonant **g** before **a**, **o**, or **u** is pronounced /g/, as in English "gas."

gato
goma
gusto

The **g** in the syllables **gue** and **gui** is pronounced /g/, as in English "guitar."

guerra
guitarra

The **gü** in the syllables **güe** and **güi** is pronounced /gw/.

vergüenza
pingüino

The consonant **g** before **e** or **i** is pronounced /h/, as in English "hint."

gente
giro

The consonant **j** sounds a bit different in Spanish. For instance, when you want to say **jamón** ("ham"), you begin to say "ham" but you make the /h/ sound harsher.

The consonant **h** is never pronounced in Spanish unless you find it in the combination **ch**, which is similar to the /ch/ in English "church."

hospital
mucho

◄ 6 ►

En el hotel
At the hotel

OBJECTIVE

In this chapter you will learn how to use direct objects, how to say "there is" and "there are," two different meanings of the verb **querer**, another way to say "I would like," some stem-changing verbs (**querer**, **poder**, **servir**, **jugar**), and some basic vocabulary about a hotel room.

◄ **6.1** ►
DIALOG 1
La habitación · *The room*

Anita and David are in their room, from which they can see a swimming pool. David says that there is also a restaurant where they serve delicious food. Anita suggests that he make a reservation to have dinner there soon because she is already hungry. Their conversation stops when she discovers that the air-conditioning does not work.

Más tarde, Anita y David hablan en la habitación. Hacen planes para ir a comer a un restaurante.

ANITA	¡Esta habitación es muy bonita! ¡Mira, hay una piscina allí!
DAVID	Sí, la veo. También, en el último piso hay un restaurante donde sirven unos platos típicos deliciosos. Además, el restaurante tiene una vista fantástica de la ciudad.
ANITA	¿Por qué no llamas y haces una reservación para ir a cenar allí esta noche?
DAVID	¿Qué hora es?
ANITA	Son las 4:10 de la tarde, hora mexicana.
DAVID	¿A qué hora quieres ir?
ANITA	Me gustaría comer a las seis. Tengo hambre ya. ¿Tienes el número de teléfono del restaurante?
DAVID	Sí, lo tengo. Ahora mismo llamo.
ANITA	¡David! ¡El aire acondicionado no funciona!

◄ **6.2** ►
Vocabulario

muy bonito(-a)	*very beautiful*
¡mira!	*look!*
hay una piscina allí	*there is a swimming pool there*
la veo (ver) (*irregular*)	*I see it*
en el último piso	*on the top floor*
tiene una vista	*it has a view*
además	*besides*
donde sirven	*where they serve*
los platos típicos deliciosos	*delicious traditional meals*
¿por qué no llamas?	*why don't you call?*
haces una reservación	*you make a reservation*

cenar	*to have dinner*
esta noche	*tonight*
ya	*already, now*
ahora mismo	*right now*
el aire acondicionado no funciona	*the air-conditioning does not work*
me gustaría	*I would like*

Vocabulario adicional

la toalla	*towel*
la almohada	*pillow*
la calefacción	*heating system*
la ventana	*window*
la puerta	*door*
la silla	*chair*
la cama	*bed*
la sábana	*sheet*
la frazada	*blanket*
la ducha	*shower*
el agua (*feminine*) fría	*cold water*
el agua (*feminine*) caliente	*hot water*
la bañera	*bathtub*
el jabón	*soap*
la pasta de dientes	*toothpaste*
el cepillo de dientes	*toothbrush*
el secador de pelo	*hair dryer*
el papel higiénico	*toilet paper*

◄ 6.3 ►
Comprensión y expresión

"I would like to"

In the dialog Anita says **me gustaría** when she tells David that she "would like" to have dinner at 6 P.M. Remember that you can also use **quisiera**. For instance, you can say either *Me gustaría* tomar un **refresco** ("cold drink") or *Quisiera* tomar un **refresco**.

"There is, there are"

Hay is the word used to express "there is" or "there are."

Hay un restaurante muy bueno en el hotel.	*There is a very good restaurant in the hotel.*
Hay tres toallas en el baño.	*There are three towels in the bathroom.*

◄ 6.4 ►
Estructura gramatical

Direct objects

A direct object is a noun or pronoun that directly receives the verb's action and answers the question "what?" or "whom?"

¿Ves la piscina?	*Do you see the pool?*
Sí, **la** veo.	*Yes, I see it.*
¿Tienes el secador de pelo?	*Do you have the hair dryer?*
No **lo** tengo.	*No, I don't have it.*

Here are the direct object pronouns.

me	Ella **me** conoce.	*She knows me.*
te	Yo **te** invito.	*I invite you.*
lo	Ana compra un libro. **Lo** compra.	*She buys it.*
la	María tiene la toalla. **La** tiene.	*She has it.*
nos	Ana **nos** conoce.	*Ana knows us.*
los	Yo compro los libros. Yo **los** compro.	*I buy them.*
las	José escribe las cartas. José **las** escribe.	*He writes them.*

◄ 6.5 ►
Audio exercise

Anita would like to do many things today. On the recording you will hear her use **me gustaría** or **quisiera**.

Quisiera ir a ese restaurante hoy.	*I would like to go to this restaurant today.*
Quisiera tomar un refresco.	*I would like a drink.*
Me gustaría nadar en la piscina.	*I would like to swim in the pool.*
Me gustaría comer a las siete.	*I would like to eat at seven.*

Now Anita asks David if he would like to do those things.

ANITA   ¿Te gustaría ir a ese restaurante hoy?
DAVID   Sí, me gustaría ir.
ANITA   ¿Te gustaría tomar un refresco?
DAVID   Sí, me gustaría tomar una limonada.
ANITA   ¿Te gustaría nadar en la piscina?
DAVID   Sí, ¡tengo mucho calor!
ANITA   ¿Te gustaría comer a las siete?
DAVID   No, quisiera comer a las seis. Tengo hambre.

◄ 6.6 ►
Exercise

Complete these questions and responses with the appropriate word(s).

1. ¿_____ gustaría ir al hotel?

   Sí, _____ gustaría, tengo sueño.

2. ¿Te _____ comer en ese restaurante?

   Sí, _____ gustaría mucho, tengo hambre.

3. ¿_____ tomar un taxi?

   No, _____ gustaría tomar el tren.

4. ¿_____ tomar un refresco?

   Sí, quisiera tomar un refresco, tengo sed.

5. ¿Te _____ ir a la piscina?

   Sí, _____ gustaría ir. Tengo calor.

◄ 6.7 ►
Audio practice

In the following conversation, Anita is pointing out to David all the nice things she sees in the hotel. Notice how she uses **hay**, which means "there is" or "there are."

ANITA   ¡David, mira, hay un balcón! (balcón, *balcony*)
DAVID   ¡Cuidado! (cuidado, *careful*)
ANITA   ¡Hay un sofá muy cómodo!
DAVID   ¡Qué bueno! ¡Tengo sueño!
ANITA   ¡Hay una piscina allí!

DAVID   ¡No tengo ganas de nadar! (nadar, *swim*)
ANITA   ¡Hay dos chocolates en la cama!
DAVID   ¡Son para mí!

Now practice saying aloud the following examples.

Hay un balcón en la habitación.	*There is a balcony in the room.*
Hay una piscina en el hotel.	*There is a pool in the hotel.*
Hay un sofá cómodo allí.	*There is a comfortable sofa there.*
Hay tres toallas en el baño.	*There are three towels in the bathroom.*
Hay muchos taxis en la calle.	*There are many taxis in the street.*

◄ 6.8 ►
Exercise

A direct object is a noun or pronoun that directly receives the verb's action, for example, **veo la piscina** ("I see the pool"). We can replace the noun with a pronoun, in this example, **la**—**la veo** ("I see it"). When we use a pronoun, we place it before the conjugated verb. Since nouns are either masculine or feminine and either singular or plural, there are four corresponding pronouns, **lo, la, los,** and **las.**

Answer the following statements in the affirmative, saying that you see it or them by using the correct direct object pronoun.

EXAMPLE   Hay una casa grande.

_____Sí, la veo._____

1. Hay dos taxis en la calle.   _____

2. Hay un refresco en la mesa.   _____

3. Hay ocho sillas aquí.   _____

4. Hay un balcón en la casa.   _____

5. Hay una señora y un niño en el hotel.

_____

6. Hay un ascensor.   _____

7. Hay una toalla en el baño.   _____

8. Hay un señor en el restaurante.

_____

◄ 6.9 ►

DIALOG 2
¡Te quiero! · *I love you!*

Anita and David went to the swimming pool for a while, and now they are going back to their room to change in order to go to the restaurant. David seems to have misplaced the key for a moment.

ANITA	¿No tienes la llave?
DAVID	Sí, ¡la tengo! ¿Tienes tu pasaporte?
ANITA	Sí, lo tengo. ¿Quieres mi pasaporte?
DAVID	No lo quiero, pero ¡te quiero!
ANITA	¿Me quieres?
DAVID	Sí, ¡te quiero!
ANITA	Entonces, ¿me puedes llevar en seguida a ese restaurante estupendo?

◄ 6.10 ►

Vocabulario

la llave	*key*
¿quieres? (querer) (e>ie)	*do you want?*
No lo quiero.	*I don't want it.*
Te quiero.	*I love you.*
¿Me quieres?	*Do you love me?*
entonces	*then*
¿me puedes llevar?	*can you take me?*
en seguida	*right away*

◄ 6.11 ►

Comprensión y expresión

The verb **querer** means "to want." In the dialog when Anita asks **¿quieres mi pasaporte?** and David answers **no *lo* quiero**, he is saying that he doesn't want it. However, when he says **pero *te* quiero**, he is saying "but I love you." When the verb **querer** is used with a direct object referring to a person, the meaning is usually "to love."

¿Quiere Ud. dos habitaciones?	*Do you want two rooms?*
No, quiero una habitación.	*No, I want one room.*

¿Qué quieres hacer?	*What do you want to do?*
Quiero ir al cine.	*I want to go to the movies.*
¿Me quieres?	*Do you love me?*
Sí, te quiero.	*Yes, I love you.*

Lovers like to find out whether they are loved by picking the petals of a flower while they say, **me quieres mucho, poquito, nada** ("you love me a lot, a little, not at all") after each petal.

◄ 6.12 ►
Estructura gramatical

Querer is a stem-changing verb, a verb that changes both the endings and the stem (the first part of the infinitive). For example, the form for "I want" is **quiero**. Notice that the stem changes in a pattern. Let's review the forms of **querer**.

yo quiero
tú quieres
él, ella, Ud. quiere
nosotros queremos
ellos, ellas, Uds. quieren

All stem-changing verbs change the stem in all forms except the **nosotros** form. All stem-changing verbs of this type (**e>ie**) follow this same pattern.

PENSAR ("to think")

ie	pienso
ie	piensas
ie	piensa
e	pensamos
ie	piensan

There are four groups of stem-changing verbs.

e>ie	**o>ue**
querer ("to want")	poder ("to be able")
pensar ("to think")	mover ("to move")
mentir ("to lie")	morir ("to die")
sentir ("to feel")	
sentar ("to sit")	

e>i   u>ue

servir ("to serve")   jugar ("to play a game")
pedir ("to request")

Let's look at how some of these verbs conjugate in the present tense.

PODER	SERVIR	JUGAR
puedo	sirvo	juego
puedes	sirves	juegas
puede	sirve	juega
podemos	servimos	jugamos
pueden	sirven	juegan

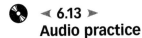

◄ 6.13 ►
Audio practice

Anita and David are using the verb **querer** in two different ways. When she says **¿Quieres mi pasaporte?** she is asking David whether he wants her passport. One of the meanings of **querer** is "to want," as in the following questions and responses. Listen to them on the recording and repeat.

¿Quieres la llave?   *Do you want the key?*
Sí, la quiero.   *Yes, I want it.*

¿Quieres dos taxis?   *Do you want two taxis?*
No, quiero un taxi.   *No, I want one taxi.*

¿Quiere Ud. jugar al tenis? *Do you want to play tennis?*
No, quiero jugar al golf.   *No, I want to play golf.*

¿Quieren Uds. ir al cine?   *Do you want to go to the movies?*
Sí, queremos ir al cine.   *Yes, we want to go to the movies.*

¿Quieren ellos ir a la piscina?   *Do they want to go to the pool?*
Sí, ellos quieren ir a la piscina. *Yes, they want to go to the pool.*

Querer also means "to love" when it is used in a different context, as in the following questions and responses on the recording.

Pablo, ¿me quieres?   *Pablo, do you love me?*
Sí, María, te quiero.   *Yes, María, I love you.*

¿Me quieres mucho?	*Do you love me a lot?*
¡Te quiero muchísimo!	*I love you a lot!*

María, ¿te quieren ellos?	*María, do they love you?*
Sí, ellos me quieren mucho.	*Yes, they love me a lot.*

¿Me quieren Uds.?	*Do you all love me?*
Sí, te queremos.	*Yes, we all love you.*

◄ 6.14 ►
DIALOG 3
¿Me puede _____? · *Can you _____ for me?*

David and Anita are getting ready to go to the restaurant, but they have some problems: the air-conditioning does not work, and they need a hair dryer.

Hay unos problemas: el aire acondicionado no funciona y no hay un secador de pelo en la habitación.

RECEPCIONISTA	¡Aló! ¿En qué puedo servirla?
ANITA	Señorita, el aire acondicionado no funciona.
RECEPCIONISTA	Lo siento mucho. El mecánico va y lo arregla en seguida.
ANITA	Gracias. ¿Me puede mandar un secador de pelo?
RECEPCIONISTA	La camarera lo lleva inmediatamente. ¿Algo más?
ANITA	Nada más, por ahora, gracias.

◄ 6.15 ►
Vocabulario

Lo siento mucho.	*I am very sorry.*
el mecánico va	*the mechanic is going*
lo arregla	*he fixes it*
en seguida	*right away*
¿me puede mandar?	*can you send me?*
el secador de pelo	*hair dryer*
¿Algo más?	*Something else?*
nada más	*nothing else*
por ahora	*for now*

◄ 6.16 ►
Comprensión y expresión

Me puede(s) or **te puedo** followed by an infinitive is the way to ask "can you _____," "can I _____," and so on.

¿Me puedes traer el secador de pelo?	*Can you bring me the hair dryer?*
Sí, te lo puedo traer.	*Yes, I can bring it to you.*
¿Te puedo hablar?	*Can I talk to you?*
Sí, me puedes hablar (puedes hablarme).	*Yes, you can talk to me.*

When the receptionist wants to apologize for the fact that the air-conditioning does not work, she says, **Lo siento mucho.** When we want to say that we are sorry, we say, **lo sentimos.** The infinitive form of the verb is **sentirlo.** We can add **mucho,** to say we are *very* sorry.

◄ 6.17 ►
Estructura gramatical

Object pronouns can be placed before the verb or attached to the end of an infinitive.

> ¿Puede mandar**me** una toalla?   *Can you send me a towel?*
> OR ¿**Me** puede mandar una toalla?

The receptionist says **¿En qué puedo servir*la*?** when she is talking to Anita, but she would say **servir*lo*** when she is talking to David. The expression literally means "How can I serve you?" The pronoun for "you" formal is **la** (feminine) or **lo** (masculine). If she were to use the informal "you," then she would say **servir*te*.**

 ## ◄ 6.18 ►
Audio practice

Keep in mind that object pronouns are used before a conjugated verb. On the recording, listen and repeat the following short conversations, noting the use of an object pronoun.

¿Tienes las toallas?	*Do you have the towels?*
Sí, las tengo.	*Yes, I have them.*
¿Tiene María la llave?	*Does María have the key?*
Sí, la tiene.	*Yes, she has it.*
¿Tienen Uds. una reservación?	*Do you have a reservation?*
Sí, la tenemos.	*Yes, we have it.*
¿Lleva la camarera el secador de pelo?	*Is the maid taking the hair dryer?*
Sí, la camarera lo lleva.	*Yes, the maid is taking it.*
¿Arregla el mecánico el aire acondicionado?	*Is the mechanic fixing the air-conditioning?*
Sí, el mecánico lo arregla.	*Yes, the mechanic is fixing it.*

 ◄ **6.19** ►
Audio practice

Object pronouns can be attached to the end of an infinitive. This provides a second way to express an object pronoun when there is an infinitive in a sentence. Listen to the recording, repeating both ways to ask the question, then write the alternate way of asking the question below.

1. El secador de pelo no funciona. ¿Lo puedes arreglar?
   The hair dryer doesn't work. Can you fix it?

   _____

2. Las bananas son deliciosas. ¿Las quieres comer?
   The bananas are delicious. Do you want to eat them?

   _____

3. Necesito mandar una carta. ¿Puedo mandarla ahora?
   I need to send a letter. Can I send it now?

   _____

4. Necesitamos tres toallas en la piscina. ¿Las puedes llevar?
   We need three towels in the pool. Can you take them?

   _____

5. Necesitamos dos botones. ¿Los puedes llamar?
   We need two bellhops. Can you call them?

   _____

◄ 6.20 ►
Audio practice

¡Me puede(s)?, followed by an infinitive, is the way to ask "Can you _____ (do something for me)?" Listen and repeat the exchanges on the recording.

¿Me puedes llamar a las tres?	Can you call me at three?
Sí, te puedo llamar a las tres.	Yes, I can call you at three.
¿Me puedes mandar la carta?	Can you send me the letter?
No, no te puedo mandar la carta.	No, I cannot send you the letter.
¿Me puedes llevar en tu coche?	Can you take me in your car?
Sí, te puedo llevar en mi coche.	Yes, I can take you in my car.
¿Me puedes presentar a María?	Can you introduce me to María?
Sí, te puedo presentar a María.	Yes, I can introduce you to María.
¿Me puedes explicar el problema?	Can you explain the problem to me?
Sí, puedo explicarte el problema.	Yes, I can explain the problem to you.

◄ 6.21 ►
Exercise

Complete the following sentences with the correct form of the verb in parentheses.

1. Ellos no _____ comer a las siete. (querer)

2. Nosotros _____ mandar la carta. (poder)

3. Tú _____ al tenis, ¿verdad? (jugar)

4. El camarero _____ los platos a la mesa. (servir)

5. Yo _____ comer en casa. (querer)

6. Uds. _____ al fútbol muy bien. (jugar)

7. Nosotros _____ en el Parque Central. (jugar)

8. La señora no _____ mover la silla. (poder)

◄ 6.22 ►
Expresión libre

Using what you have learned in this chapter, answer the speaker in a spontaneous conversation. To answer the questions posed, you'll need to use object pronouns.

◄ 6.23 ►
¡Viva la diferencia!

• What time do people eat breakfast, lunch, and dinner in Spanish-speaking countries? Breakfast (**desayuno**) is usually served at about seven in the morning. Lunch (**almuerzo**) is served between one and three in the afternoon, and dinner (**cena**) is served between eight and nine in the evening. As a matter of fact, in Spain dinner is usually very late, sometimes at ten or eleven. In many Spanish-speaking countries, tea and sandwiches are served at 5 o'clock.

• Did you know that chocolate was emperor Moctezuma's favorite drink? The Aztec emperor offered Cortés a cup of hot chocolate when they first met.

◄ 6.24 ►
How to make it sound Spanish

The consonant **q** is used only in the combination **qu**, which has the sound /k/. The combination **qu** is always followed by **e** or **i**: **que** or **qui** (**queso**, **quiero**). Don't forget this when you pronounce the name **Velázquez**; it should sound like /velázkez/.

The consonant **l** has the same sound as the English "l." However, **ll** has a different sound, similar to the /y/ sound in the word "yes." For example, **llave** is pronounced /yave/. This sound may vary in some countries, such as Argentina and Uruguay, where it is pronounced more harshly, almost as /ch/. So a **llama** (an animal from South America) is not a **lama** (a monk from Tibet). Be sure to clearly differentiate /yama/ and /lama/.

The consonant **r** is pronounced much like the /d/ sound in the word "ladder." However, **r** at the beginning of a word and **rr** are pronounced with a strong trill produced by vibrating the tip of the tongue while air passes through the mouth. The word **caro** ("expensive") is pronounced /kado/, but in order to pronounce the words **Rosa** and **carro** ("car"), you need to roll the **r** just a bit. Practice saying **caro** and **carro** until you hear the difference. Then you will be able to say **No quiero un carro caro**.

‹ 7 ›

En el restaurante

At the restaurant

OBJECTIVE

In this chapter you will learn how to use the indirect object, reflexive verbs, and pronouns that follow prepositions; how to express the future by using the verb "to go" + an infinitive; and the use of the verb **estar**. You will also become acquainted with vocabulary used in a restaurant.

DIALOG 1
¿Qué desean pedir? · *What would you like to have?*

Our friends are at a restaurant, sitting near the balcony, talking to the waiter. He tells them that the special today is grilled fillet of hake with mixed vegetables. They order two margaritas, one without salt, and a portion of guacamole with some tortillas.

David y Anita van al restaurante El Angel. Se sientan en una mesa cerca de una ventana y le hablan al mozo.

MOZO	Muy buenas tardes, señores. ¿Qué desean pedir?
DAVID Y ANITA	Buenas tardes.
ANITA	Queremos cenar.
MOZO	Aquí tienen el menú. El plato especial de hoy es filete de merluza a la plancha con verduras surtidas. ¿Desean beber algo antes de la comida?
DAVID	Anita, ¿por qué no pides una margarita?
ANITA	Sí, me gustaría una margarita sin sal, con algo para picar.
DAVID	Queremos dos margaritas, una sin sal y la otra con sal. Y nos trae una porción de guacamole con unas tortillas.
MOZO	En seguida les traigo las margaritas y el guacamole con las tortillas.

(El mozo vuelve después de unos minutos y les sirve las margaritas y el guacamole.)

Vocabulario

se sientan (sentarse) (e>ie)	*they sit down*
la mesa	*table*
el mozo	*waiter*
¿Qué desean pedir?	*What would you like to have?*
el menú	*menu*
el plato especial de hoy	*today's special*
filete de merluza	*fillet of hake*
a la plancha	*grilled*
con	*with*
las verduras surtidas	*mixed vegetables*
desean (desear)	*you wish, you want*

beber	*to drink*
antes de la comida	*before the meal*
¿por qué no pides _____?	*why don't you ask for _____?*
sin sal	*without salt*
algo para picar	*something to nibble*
la otra	*the other one*
nos trae	*you bring us*
una porción de	*a portion of*
les traigo	*I'll bring you*
vuelve (volver) (o>ue)	*he comes back*
les sirve	*he serves them*

Vocabulario adicional

las comidas	*meals*

Para el desayuno — *For breakfast*

el cereal con leche	*cereal with milk*
el pan tostado con mantequilla	*toast and butter*
la mermelada	*marmalade*
los huevos revueltos	*scrambled eggs*
los huevos fritos	*fried eggs*
con tocino	*with bacon*
el café, el té, el chocolate	*coffee, tea, hot chocolate*
el jugo de naranja	*orange juice*
la manzana	*apple*
el pomelo	*grapefruit*

Para el almuerzo — *For lunch*

la sopa de pollo/de verduras	*chicken/vegetable soup*
un sandwich de jamón y queso	*a ham and cheese sandwich*
el atún	*tuna*
el pavo	*turkey*
una hamburguesa con queso	*a cheeseburger*
las papitas	*potato chips*
una ensalada de tomate y lechuga	*a lettuce and tomato salad*

Para la cena — *For dinner*

la carne asada con puré de papas	*roast beef with mashed potatoes*

el pescado frito con papas cocidas	*fried fish with boiled potatoes*
los camarones	*shrimp (Latin America)*
los camarones a la plancha con arroz	*grilled shrimp with rice*
los tallarines con salsa de tomate	*spaghetti with tomato sauce*

De postre	*For dessert*
la fruta	*fruit*
los pasteles	*pastries*

Expresiones idiomáticas

Although we say **para el desayuno** ("for breakfast"), **para el almuerzo** ("for lunch"), **para la cena** ("for dinner"), **para el postre** ("for dessert"), we can also say **de postre** ("as dessert"), **de desayuno**, **de almuerzo**, etc.

◄ 7.3 ►
Comprensión y expresión

When the waiter asks our friends **¿qué desean pedir?** (literally, "what do you wish to ask for?"), he is really asking "what would you like to have?", which is what we usually hear in English. The answer usually begins with **quisiera, quisiéramos, me gustaría, nos gustaría, quiero, queremos**, etc.

◄ 7.4 ►
Estructura gramatical
Indirect objects

An indirect object is a word or a phrase that tells *to whom* or *for whom* something is done. The indirect object pronouns are **me, te, le, nos, les.**

David **le** habla **al mozo**.	*David is speaking to the waiter.*
Nosotros **les** explicamos el problema **a ellos**.	*We are explaining the problem to them.*

The verb traer

Traer is an irregular verb meaning "to bring." Be careful not to confuse it with **llevar**, "to take along with you." For instance, if we want to say "the waiter brings the menu to our table," we say

el camarero *trae* **el menú a nuestra mesa**. Here are the forms for the verb **traer**.

traigo
traes
trae
traemos
traen

You can see that only the first-person singular is irregular.

The verb **volver**

Volver is a stem-changing verb (**o>ue**).

VOLVER ("to return")

vuelvo
vuelves
vuelve
volvemos
vuelven

Another verb with the same **o>ue** stem change is **dormir**.

DORMIR ("to sleep")

duermo
duermes
duerme
dormimos
duermen

The verb **pedir**

Pedir is also a stem-changing verb (**e>i**). **Pedir** means "to ask for," so you don't need to follow it with a preposition. If you want to say "I ask for a reservation," you say **Pido una reservación**. Here are the forms for **pedir**.

pido
pides
pide
pedimos
piden

Another verb with the same e>i stem change is **repetir**.

REPETIR ("to repeat")

repito
repites
repite
repetimos
repiten

Reflexive verbs

Anita and David **se sientan** ("sit down") at a table. Literally, this means that "they sit themselves." A verb whose subject is both the performer and recipient of the action is called a reflexive verb. Anita and David are performing the act of sitting, and they are also the recipients of the sitting. Reflexive verbs are therefore conjugated with reflexive pronouns, which are similar to object pronouns (except for the third person).

The reflexive pronouns are **me**, **te**, **se**, **nos**, **os**, **se**. Where are these pronouns placed in a sentence?

WITH AN INFINITIVE	Quiero sentar**me** allí.
	OR **Me** quiero sentar allí.
WITH A CONJUGATED VERB	**Me** siento en esa silla y **te**
	sientas en ésta.

Here are the forms for **sentarse** and for another reflexive verb, **dormirse**. Note that **dormir** without the reflexive pronoun means "to sleep."

SENTARSE ("to sit down")	DORMIRSE ("to fall asleep")
me siento	me duermo
te sientas	te duermes
se sienta	se duerme
nos sentamos	nos dormimos
se sientan	se duermen

Two regular reflexive verbs are **lavarse** ("to wash oneself") and **secarse** ("to dry oneself").

◄ 7.5 ►
Audio practice

Sometimes the subject is both the performer and the recipient of the verb's action. We heard in the dialog that Anita and David *se sientan* **en una mesa**. This means literally that they sit themselves at a table. For instance, when we say **Me lavo las manos** ("I wash my hands"), we use **me** to say that "I wash *myself*." If I wash something else, I don't use **me**. For instance, "I wash the car" is **Lavo el auto**.

In this conversation, Anita is talking to David, who seems to be very tired.

ANITA   ¿Quieres sentarte un momento?
DAVID   Quisiera sentarme, pero necesito lavarme y secarme las
         manos. (manos, *hands*)
ANITA   ¡Rápido, por favor, no quiero dormirme!

On the recording, listen to and repeat the following examples of reflexive infinitives.

Quiero secarme.	*I want to dry myself.*
¿Deseas sentarte?	*Would you like to sit down?*
Prefiere sentarse.	*He prefers to sit down.*
Queremos lavarnos.	*We want to wash.*
Desean dormirse.	*They would like to go to sleep.*

On the recording, listen to and repeat the following examples of conjugated reflexive verbs.

Yo me siento aquí.	*I am sitting down here.*
Tú te duermes a las diez.	*You fall asleep at ten.*
Carlos se lava las manos.	*Carlos washes his hands.*
María se sienta en el sofá.	*María is sitting on the sofa.*
Nosotros nos dormimos tarde.	*We fall asleep late.*
Ellos se duermen a las 11:30.	*They fall asleep at 11:30.*
Uds. se sientan allí.	*You are sitting there.*

◄ 7.6 ►
Exercise

Complete the following sentences with the correct reflexive pronoun.

1. Elena _____ lava el pelo.

2. Nosotros _____ sentamos en la sala.

3. Carlos y Esteban _____ duermen muy tarde.

4. Ud. _____ sienta en esa silla.

5. Tú _____ secas con esa toalla.

6. Yo _____ lavo las manos.

7. Uds. _____ duermen a las 10 de la noche.

◄ 7.7 ►
Exercise

Complete the following sentences with the correct form of the reflexive verb in parentheses.

1. La señora no _____ en la cama. (sentarse) (cama, *bed*)

2. Yo _____ frecuentemente a las once. (dormirse)

3. Ellos _____ cerca de la ventana. (sentarse)

4. Nosotros _____ por un momento. (sentarse)

5. Uds. no _____ a las nueve. (dormirse)

6. Ud. _____ inmediatamente. (dormirse)

7. Juan _____ las manos. (lavarse)

8. Tú no _____ la cara. (secarse) (cara, *face*)

9. Nosotros _____ a las 11:30. (dormirse)

10. Elena y yo _____ en el sofá. (sentarse)

◄ **7.8** ►
Audio practice

An indirect object is a word or a phrase that tells *to whom* or *for whom* something is done, for instance, "I talk to them." Notice that although the direct object pronoun replaces the object itself, **Yo leo** *el libro* (**Yo** *lo* **leo**), the indirect object pronoun does not. If a sentence has an indirect object, it will also have an indirect object pronoun. For example, in the sentence **Yo** *les* **hablo** *a mis amigos* ("I talk to my friends"), you cannot say **Yo hablo** *a mis amigos*. You must say **Yo** *les* **hablo** *a mis amigos*.

Here are the indirect object pronouns.

me	*to me, for me*
te	*to you, for you (familiar)*
le	*to him, to her, to you (formal), for him, for her, for you (formal)*
nos	*to us, for us*
les	*to them, to you (plural), for them, for you (plural)*

These pronouns are used in the same way as the direct object pronouns, that is, they are placed before a conjugated verb and can be attached to an infinitive.

Elena le habla a Juan.	*Elena is talking to Juan.*
Yo les hablo a mis amigos.	*I am talking to my friends.*
Quiero hablarles a ellos.	*I want to talk to them.*

On the recording, practice the use of indirect object pronouns in the following questions and responses.

¿Me hablas a mí?	*Are you talking to me?*
Sí, te hablo a ti.	*Yes, I am talking to you.*
¿Le traes una silla a él?	*Are you bringing a chair for him?*
No le traigo una silla a él, le traigo la silla a ella.	*I am not bringing a chair for him, I am bringing the chair for her.*
¿Nos explicas tú el problema?	*Are you explaining the problem to us?*
No, Carlos les explica el problema a Uds.	*No, Carlos is explaining the problem to you.*

¿Te hablan en inglés?	*Are they speaking to you in English?*
No, me hablan en español.	*No, they are speaking to me in Spanish.*
¿Les pides permiso a ellos?	*Are you asking them for permission?*
Sí, les pido permiso.	*Yes, I am asking them for permission.*
¿Le vas a pedir su llave a Juan?	*Are you going to ask Juan for his key?*
No, voy a pedirle la llave a ella.	*No, I am going to ask her for the key.*

◄ 7.9 ►
DIALOG 2
¿Qué desean comer? · *What would you like to eat?*

Soon the waiter returns to Anita and David to take their order.

(más tarde)

MOZO   ¿Qué desean comer?

ANITA   Quisiera chiles en salsa de nueces y de postre, helado de fresa.

DAVID   ¿Qué sopas tienen?

MOZO   Tenemos sopa de frijoles, de pollo y fideos y de tomate.

DAVID   Voy a tomar sopa de tomate, tamales con picadillo de pollo y de postre, ¿qué me recomienda?

MOZO   Tenemos piña rellena con cerezas, helados y flan.

DAVID   Voy a probar la piña rellena. Además, media botella de vino blanco.

(El mozo anota el pedido y se va. Unos minutos más tarde regresa con el vino, abre la botella y lo sirve.)

◄ 7.10 ►
Vocabulario

la salsa de nueces	*walnut sauce*
de postre	*for dessert*
el helado de fresa	*strawberry ice cream*
la sopa de frijoles	*bean soup*

la sopa de pollo y fideos	*chicken noodle soup*
la sopa de tomate	*tomato soup*
el picadillo de pollo	*chicken hash*
la piña rellena	*stuffed pineapple*
probar	*to try*
además	*besides, moreover*
media botella	*half a bottle*
el vino blanco	*white wine*
anota (anotar)	*he writes down*
el pedido	*order*
regresa (regresar)	*he comes back, he returns*
abre (abrir)	*he opens*
lo sirve	*he serves it*

Vocabulario adicional

el vino tinto	*red wine*
la cerveza	*beer*
las tapas	*hors d'oeuvres (Spain)*
las gambas	*shrimp (Spain)*
las gambas a la plancha	*grilled shrimp*
las papitas	*potato chips*
el cuchillo	*knife*
el tenedor	*fork*
la cuchara	*spoon*
la cucharita	*teaspoon*
la servilleta	*napkin*
el vaso	*glass*
la silla	*chair*
dejar propina	*to leave a tip*
pescados y mariscos	*fish and shellfish*
la langosta	*lobster*
las almejas	*clams*
los mejillones	*mussels*
el cangrejo	*crab*
un brindis	*a toast*
brindar	*to toast (in honor of)*
el bistec	*beefsteak*
casi crudo	*rare*
término medio	*medium rare*
bien cocido	*well done*

◀ 7.11 ▶
Estructura gramatical

Prepositions + pronouns

The following pronouns are used with prepositions. You will notice that most are personal pronouns, except for the first- and second-person singular.

para	mí
por	ti
en	él, ella, Ud.
de	nosotros
a	ellos, ellas, Uds.
con	(*except* con + mí, conmigo; con + ti, contigo)

Esta silla es **para Ud.**	*This chair is for you.*
Quiero ir **contigo.**	*I want to go with you.*
Lo hago **por ti.**	*I am doing it for you (for your sake).*
Le hablo **a ella.**	*I speak to her.*

The verb ir

When David says **Voy a tomar sopa de tomate**, he is saying, "I am going to have tomato soup." Later he says, **Voy a probar la piña rellena**, "I am going to try the stuffed pineapple." He is using the verb "to go" followed by an infinitive to express a future action, just as we do in English. As you can see, the verb "to go," besides meaning to move to a different place, is also used to express the future.

Here are the forms for the verb **ir** ("to go").

voy
vas
va
vamos
van

The verb **ir** ("to go"), similar to English, is usually followed by the preposition **a** ("to").

Voy a Guatemala.	*I am going to Guatemala.*
¿**Vas a** casa?	*Are you going home?*

When we use the verb **ir** to express the future, we use it with an infinitive.

Voy a comer allí.	*I am going to eat there.*
Vamos a hablar con ella.	*We are going to speak with her.*

 ◄ 7.12 ►
Audio practice

Look at the following examples using the verb **ir** followed by an infinitive to express the future.

Vamos a comer a las siete.	*We are going to eat at seven.*
¿Vas a hablar con ellos?	*Are you going to speak with them?*
Voy a ir al cine esta tarde.	*I am going to go to the movies this evening.*
María va a beber vino blanco.	*María is going to drink white wine.*
Ellos van a comer almejas fritas.	*They are going to eat fried clams.*

Of course we can also use the verb **ir** when we want to say that we go somewhere.

¿Vas a casa de tus amigos?	*Are you going to your friends' house?*
Voy a Acapulco en marzo.	*I am going to Acapulco in March.*
Eduardo va a la escuela a las ocho.	*Eduardo goes to school at eight.*
Vamos a ese restaurante esta noche.	*We are going to that restaurant tonight.*
Mis amigos van a España este verano.	*My friends are going to Spain this summer.*

 ◄ 7.13 ►
Audio practice

Prepositions are used with personal pronouns, but the first- and second-person singular pronouns have special forms: **mí, ti.** Look at the following examples.

La sopa es **para mí**.	*The soup is for me.*
El cangrejo es **para ti**.	*The crab is for you.*
El bistec es **para ella**.	*The beefsteak is for her.*
Ellos hablan **de él**.	*They are speaking about him.*
Nosotros pensamos **en Uds.**	*We are thinking about you.*
Yo les hablo **a ellos**.	*I am speaking to them.*

However, when we use the preposition **con** ("with"), the first- and second-person singular forms are **conmigo** and **contigo**.

¿Vas **conmigo** al concierto?	Are you going with me to the concert?
Sí, voy **contigo**.	Yes, I am going with you.
¿Va Juanita **con él**?	Is Juanita going with him?
Juanita va **con nosotros**.	Juanita is going with us.
Sí, ella va **con Uds**.	Yes, she is going with you.

On the recording, listen and then repeat the following sentences to practice using prepositions and pronouns.

Este sombrero es para Elena.	*This hat is for Elena.*
Esas servilletas son para ellos.	*Those napkins are for them.*
Esta cucharita es para mí.	*This teaspoon is for me.*
Esa corbata es para ti, David.	*That tie is for you, David.*
Estos vasos son para nosotros.	*These glasses are for us.*

On the recording you will also hear Anita and David make plans for the afternoon. Listen and then repeat so you can learn how to use "with" and a pronoun.

ANITA   David, ¿quieres ir conmigo al museo esta tarde?

DAVID   Sí, quiero ir contigo, y María quiere ir con nosotros.

ANITA   ¡Qué bueno! Quiero ir con ella.

◄ 7.14 ►
Exercise

Complete the following sentences in Spanish using the prepositions and pronouns indicated at the end of each sentence.

1. Esa cuchara es _____. *(for her)*

2. El queso es _____. *(for us)*

3. El cuchillo es _____. *(for you, formal)*

4. Vamos a Venezuela _____. *(with them)*

5. Quiero ir _____. *(with you, familiar)*

6. Queremos comer _____. *(with them)*

7. ¿Vas a ir _____? *(with me)*

 ◄ **7.15** ►

DIALOG 3

¿Dejamos propina? · *Do we leave a tip?*

Our friends have finished their meal and they are about to pay their bill. Listen to how they discuss whether they should leave a tip, since very often Latin American restaurants give you a bill with the service included.

David y Anita han terminado de comer y se preparan para pagar la cuenta.

DAVID	¡Mozo! La cuenta por favor.
MOZO	¿Va a pagar en efectivo o con tarjeta de crédito?
DAVID	¿Qué tarjetas aceptan?
MOZO	Aceptamos todas las tarjetas.
DAVID	Muy bien, aquí está mi tarjeta.

(Unos minutos más tarde el mozo les trae la cuenta.)

ANITA	¿Está incluido el servicio?
DAVID	Pues, no sé. Voy a ver en esta otra cuenta detallada. ¡Ah! Aquí está. El servicio está incluido, entonces no tenemos que dejar propina.

◄ **7.16** ►

Vocabulario

la cuenta	*the bill*
pagar en efectivo	*to pay cash*
aceptan (aceptar)	*you accept*
¿Está incluido el servicio?	*Is the service included?*
Voy a ver	*I am going to see*
esta otra cuenta detallada	*this other detailed bill*
entonces	*then*
no tenemos que	*we don't have to*
dejar propina	*leave a tip*

Vocabulario adicional

el café con leche	*coffee and milk*
el café espreso	*espresso*
un bajativo	*an after-dinner drink*
el quince por ciento	*15%*
el total	*total*

| el cambio | *change* |
| No tengo cambio | *I don't have change* |

◄ 7.17 ►
Estructura gramatical

The verb estar

David says **aquí** *está* **mi tarjeta**, meaning "here is my card." Then he says **el servicio** *está* **incluido**, meaning "the service is included." This is another Spanish verb that means "to be." When you want to give a location, such as "here is my card" or "we are at the theater," you use the verb **estar**. You also use this verb with a past participle, as in "it *is included*" or "they *are served*," when you are talking about a temporary state, such as the meals that are already served at the table.

Here are the forms of the verb **estar**.

> estoy
> estás
> está
> estamos
> están

◄ 7.18 ►
Audio practice

On the recording, practice the following questions and answers, using **estar** ("to be") to express location.

¿Dónde estás?
Estoy en casa.

¿Dónde está tu casa?
Mi casa está en la calle Molina N° 25.

¿Estás contento hoy?
Sí, estoy contento, porque Juanita está conmigo.

¿Están preparados Uds. para ir a la fiesta?
Sí, estamos preparados.

◄ 7.19 ►
Exercise

Complete the following sentences with the correct form of **estar**.

1. Yo _____ en Acapulco ahora.

2. Ellos _____ en casa de Juan.

3. Ud. no _____ en su casa.

4. Nosotros _____ cansados. (cansados, *tired*)

5. Uds. _____ dormidos. (dormidos, *asleep*)

6. Tú _____ en el gimnasio.

7. El museo _____ en la calle 82.

8. Verónica _____ sentada. (sentada, *sitting*)

9. Carlota y Elena _____ cansadas.

10. El Sr. González _____ dormido.

◄ 7.20 ►
Expresión libre

Using what you have learned in this chapter, answer the speaker in a spontaneous conversation about food and drink.

◄ 7.21 ►
Pitfall

¿Ser o estar? · *Which verb "to be"?*

Listen to the recording as a student asks the teacher about something she has not understood clearly concerning the use of **ser** and **estar**.

The student wanted to know how to give a location, "I am at home." The correct verb to use is **estar** when we want to give a location, so the teacher explains that **estoy en casa** is correct. The student is then not sure whether to use **ser** or **estar** when she wants to express a condition, "I am sad." The teacher explains that the correct way to say this is **estoy triste**. We use **estar** when we want to express a condition.

◄ 7.22 ►
¡Viva la diferencia!

• Lunch is the most important meal in Hispanic countries. Dinner is a rather light meal and is generally served very late, especially in Spain, where it can be as late as eleven at night.

• Spaniards like to go to a café between five and nine in the evening to talk with their friends, eat tapas, and drink a glass of wine or a beer. **Tapas** may be **chorizo** ("sausage"), **aceitunas** ("olives"), **tortilla española** ("potato omelet"), **queso** ("cheese"), **sardinas** ("sardines"), etc.

• Here is a recipe for a popular Spanish drink.

Sangría

INGREDIENTES
Vino tinto
Jugo de fruta
Fruta: naranjas (*oranges*), duraznos (*peaches*) o fresas (*strawberries*)
Vermut

PREPARACIÓN
Se mezcla (*mix*) un poco (*a small amount*) de vermut con el vino tinto y un poco de jugo de fruta. Se le agrega (*add*) la fruta que Ud. prefiera.

◄ 7.23 ►
Situaciones

Imagine that you are in the following situations. Try to respond aloud, practicing until your reply is fluent.

1. You and two friends go to a restaurant in Mexico D.F. for lunch. The waiter cannot understand one of your friends. Help your friend order a soup, a main dish, and a dessert. Ask the waiter if they have any specials, order a main dish and dessert for yourself, and order drinks for you and your friends.

2. You and a friend are in a café in Madrid. Order something to drink and some tapas.

3. You go to a restaurant and order for you and your two children. Your daughter (**hija**) does not eat meat.

4. You are having a party. You offer two different main dishes, three beverages, and two desserts.

5. You are a waiter/waitress. Greet the people at a table, offer them five different specials you have today in your restaurant, and ask them if they want anything to drink.

◄ 7.24 ►
How to make it sound Spanish

The consonant **x** has two pronunciations.

When **x** is between vowels, the sound is similar to /ks/, as in English "taxes."

examen   /eksamen/

When **x** is before a consonant, the sound is /s/.

excusa   /eskusa/

The consonant **ñ** is pronounced like the English combination *ny* in the word "canyon."

niño   /ninyo/

◄ *8* ►

Por la ciudad
Around the city

OBJECTIVE

In this chapter you will become acquainted with the vocabulary and phrases used to express an obligation, comparisons of inequality, and how to book a tour, go shopping, and bargain. You will also learn the differences between **ser** and **estar** ("to be") and between **saber** and **conocer** ("to know").

⊙ ◄ **8.1** ►
DIALOG 1
México D.F. · *Mexico City*

Our friends have seen many interesting places in Mexico City during the day. They went to Frida Kahlo's house, then to the Zona Rosa, an elegant section downtown, where they had lunch. In the afternoon they went to the Chapultepec Castle and the Museum of Anthropology. Finally, they went to the Palacio de Bellas Artes, a beautiful theater, to buy tickets to see the Ballet Folklórico Mexicano. Back at the hotel they are resting before going to the performance. Listen to them making plans to go to the theater.

David y Anita salen a dar un paseo por la ciudad. Primero van a la casa de Frida Kahlo; después van a la Zona Rosa donde almuerzan; y por la tarde van al Castillo de Chapultepec y al Museo de Antropología. Finalmente, van al Palacio de Bellas Artes para comprar entradas para ver el Ballet Folklórico Mexicano esa noche. De vuelta en el hotel, descansan un poco antes de ir a la función del Ballet Folklórico.

DAVID ¿A qué hora comienza la función del Ballet Folklórico?

ANITA A las nueve de la noche, pero hay que llegar unos 15 minutos antes. Tenemos bastante tiempo. ¿Quieres cenar antes de la función o después?

DAVID Si no te importa, podemos hacerlo antes de la función.

ANITA Hay un restaurante muy bueno cerca del Palacio de Bellas Artes. La guía turística dice que es el mejor restaurante típico de la ciudad. Estoy segura de que tenemos que hacer una reservación. ¿Por qué no llamas?

DAVID Muy buena idea. ¿Sabes? Creo que es mejor tomar el metro, ya que el restaurante está muy cerca del teatro.

ANITA ¡Por supuesto! Vamos a ir muy rápido en el metro; pero antes, tengo que descansar. Con tanto caminar, ¡me duelen horriblemente los pies!

DAVID Para ver la ciudad, hay que caminar.

ANITA Sí, hay que caminar, ¡pero no hay que exagerar!

◄ 8.2 ►
Vocabulario

salen (salir) (*irregular*)	*they go out*
dar un paseo	*to take a stroll*
almuerzan (almorzar) (o>ue)	*they have lunch*
las entradas	*tickets*
de vuelta	*back*
descansan (descansar)	*they rest*
un poco	*a little*
la función	*performance*
comienza (comenzar) (e>ie)	*it begins*
si no te importa	*if it makes no difference to you*
antes de	*before*
estoy segura	*I am sure*
tenemos que hacer	*we have to make*
hacer (*irregular*)	*to do, to make*
creo (creer)	*I believe*
es mejor	*it is better, best*
tomar el metro	*to take the subway*
está muy cerca	*it is very close, near*
por supuesto	*of course*
tengo que descansar	*I have to rest*
con tanto caminar	*with so much walking*
me duelen los pies	*my feet are hurting*
para ver	*in order to see*
hay que caminar	*one must walk*
no hay que exagerar	*one must not overdo it*

Expresión idiomática

por supuesto	*of course*

◄ 8.3 ►
Comprensión y expresión

Public transportation

David says **es mejor tomar el metro** when he tells Anita that it is better to take the subway. Here are some other expressions used for transportation.

tomar el tren	*to take the train*
tomar el autobús	*to take the bus*
tomar un taxi	*to take a taxi*

In many countries, besides the common vehicles mentioned above, there is a fast and inexpensive means of transportation, **el colectivo**, usually a small car that takes three or four people for a flat rate. They are faster because they stop only as requested, so if the passengers travel a long distance, the **colectivo** doesn't stop until it reaches the first destination. There it may pick up a new passenger, or it may continue until someone stops it for a ride.

"It hurts me, it pleases me"

When David says **si no te importa**, and later Anita says **me duelen horriblemente los pies**, they are using verbs that have a special construction: **gustar, importar, doler, molestar**, etc. These verbs are used in a different way. For instance, **me gusta** does not mean "I like," but rather "it pleases me."

Me gusta la habitación.	*I like the room. (The room pleases me.)*
Te duele la cabeza.	*You have a headache. (Your head is hurting you.)*
A Anita no le importa.	*It makes no difference to Anita.*
Me molestan esos zapatos.	*Those shoes bother me.*

◄ 8.4 ►
Audio practice

The verbs **gustar** ("to like"), **doler** ("to hurt"), **molestar** ("to bother"), and **importar** ("to matter") are used in a different way. Notice how David and Anita use these verbs in the following conversation.

DAVID   ¿Te gustaría ir a cenar a las seis?

ANITA   No me importa, porque me gusta cenar temprano.

DAVID   ¿Te molesta ir antes de las seis?

ANITA   Sí, me molesta, porque quiero descansar. ¡Me duelen los pies!

DAVID   ¡Pero, te gusta caminar!

ANITA   Me gusta caminar, ¡pero no me gusta exagerar!

Anita thinks that they walked too much. She likes to walk, but she doesn't like to overdo it. On the other hand, it does not matter to her if they go to dinner at six.

On the recording, listen and repeat the following exchanges.

¿Te gustan los bailarines? *Do you like the dancers?*
Sí, me gustan mucho. *Yes, I like them a lot.*

¿Le molesta a Anita caminar? *Does walking bother Anita?*
No, a Anita no le molesta *No, walking doesn't bother Anita,*
　caminar, le molesta exagerar. *but overdoing it bothers her.*

¿Les importa a Uds. ir más *Does it make any difference to*
　tarde? *you to go later?*
No, no nos importa ir más tarde. *No, it doesn't make any difference*
to us to go later.

¿Te duelen los pies? *Do your feet hurt?*
Sí, me duelen mucho porque *Yes, they hurt a lot because I walk*
　camino mucho. *a lot.*

¿Te duele la cabeza? *Does your head hurt?*
Sí, me duele la cabeza. Necesito *Yes, my head hurts. I need an*
　una aspirina. *aspirin.*

¿Te importa comer en ese *Does it make any difference to*
　restaurante? *you to eat in that restaurant?*
No me importa, pero a Anita *No, it doesn't make any difference*
　le importa. *to me, but it makes a difference*
to Anita.

◄ 8.5 ►
Exercise

Answer the following questions.

1. ¿Por qué quieres tomar dos aspirinas?

　_____

2. ¿Qué te van a doler si caminas mucho?

　_____

3. ¿Te molesta limpiar la casa?

　_____

4. ¿Les importa a tus amigos ir en autobús?

　_____

5. ¿Qué te duele si comes mucho? (el estómago, *stomach*)

　_____

6. ¿Le importa a Ud. comer tarde?

_____

7. ¿Les molesta a Uds. caminar a casa?

_____

◄ 8.6 ►
Comprensión y expresión

When Anita says that she is sure that they *have to make* a reservation, she says **estoy segura de que tenemos que hacer una reservación.** When you want to express an obligation, you use **tener que** + infinitive.

Tengo que ir a las ocho de la mañana.	*I have to go at eight in the morning.*
Tenemos que caminar rápidamente.	*We have to walk fast.*

But if you want to make an impersonal statement, use **hay que** + infinitive. That's why our friends say **Hay que llegar unos 15 minutos antes** (not only David and Anita, but everybody going to the theater should arrive 15 minutes early), **hay que caminar, no hay que exagerar.**

◄ 8.7 ►
Audio practice

In Spanish, we use the verb **tener que** followed by an infinitive when we want to express an obligation—for instance, **Tengo que ir a la biblioteca** ("I have to go to the library"). However, if the need or obligation pertains to everyone, we say **hay que**— for instance, **Hay que comer para vivir** ("One must eat in order to live"). Let's see what Anita and David have to do when they get back to the States.

ANITA   David, ¿tienes que hablar con José el sábado?

DAVID   No, tengo que hablar con Joaquín. ¿Y tú?

ANITA   ¡Tengo que descansar! ¿Qué tienen que hacer tú y Mario?

DAVID   Tenemos que ir a cenar con Joaquín. Tiene que darnos el informe. (informe, *report*)

ANITA   ¡Ah! ¡Ahora recuerdo que tengo que escribir un informe también!

DAVID   ¡Hay que trabajar!

Practice and repeat the following exchanges on the recording.

¿Qué tienes que hacer hoy?	*What do you have to do today?*
Tengo que ir a la biblioteca.	*I have to go to the library.*
¿Qué tienen que hacer Uds. esta tarde?	*What do you have to do this afternoon?*
Tenemos que escribir unas tarjetas.	*We have to write some postcards.*
¿Qué tiene que hacer Ud. esta noche?	*What do you have to do tonight?*
Tengo que ir al concierto de la filarmónica.	*I have to go to the Philharmonic concert.*
¿Qué hay que hacer hoy?	*What must be done today?*
Hay que preparar el informe de este mes.	*This month's report must be prepared.*
¿Hay que vivir para comer?	*Must one live to eat?*
¡No, hay que comer para vivir!	*No, one must eat to live!*

◄ 8.8 ►
Exercise

Complete the following sentences with the correct form of **tener que** or **hay que**.

1. Yo _____ ir a la escuela.

2. Ella _____ hacer su tarea. (tarea, *homework*)

3. Uds. _____ dormir más.

4. Nosotros _____ hablar con la profesora.

5. Tú _____ sentarte aquí.

6. _____ estudiar para aprender.

7. _____ comer para vivir.

◄ 8.9 ►
Estructura gramatical

Adverbs

Adverbs are formed by adding **-mente** to the feminine form of the adjective.

rápido (*masculine*)	*rapid*
rápida (*feminine*)	*rapid*
rápidamente	*rapidly*

IRREGULAR ADVERBS

bien	*well*
mal	*badly*

Comparisons of inequality

To compare two different things, use **más** + adjective + **que** or **menos** + adjective + **que**.

Carlos es **más** alto **que** yo. (alto[-a], *tall*)
Ese hotel es **menos** caro **que** éste. (caro[-a], *expensive*)

IRREGULAR FORMS

mejor	*better*
peor	*worse*
mayor	*older*
menor	*younger*

Este restaurante es **mejor**   *This restaurant is better than*
  que ése.   *that one.*

Superlatives

To express a superlative, we use **el** or **la** + **más** or **menos** (or one of the irregular forms) + adjective + **de**.

El Prado es **el** museo **más**   *The Prado is the most important*
  importante **de** Madrid.   *museum in Madrid.*
Ella es **la** estudiante **más**   *She is the most intelligent*
  inteligente **de** la clase.   *student in the class.*
Fernando es **el mayor de**   *Fernando is the oldest in the*
  la familia.   *family.*
Benjamín es **el menor de**   *Benjamin is the youngest of his*
  sus hermanos.   *brothers.*

◄ **8.10** ►
Audio practice

Comparatives and superlatives

In the following conversation, Anita and David compare places they have seen in México City. Notice their use of comparatives and superlatives.

ANITA   ¿Crees que la casa de Frida Kahlo es más interesante que el Museo Antropológico?

DAVID   Creo que la casa de Frida Kahlo es más interesante porque me gusta más el arte.

ANITA   ¿Piensas que el Palacio de Bellas Artes es menos importante que la Zona Rosa?

DAVID   Pienso que el Palacio de Bellas Artes es más importante.

ANITA   ¡Es el teatro más hermoso de la ciudad! (hermoso, *beautiful*)

On the recording, practice the following sentences.

Mi bicicleta es más vieja que tu bicicleta.	*My bicycle is older than your bicycle.*
Carlos es más alto que Juan.	*Carlos is taller than Juan.*
Catalina es más simpática que Elena.	*Catalina is nicer than Elena.*
Esta casa es menos grande que ésa.	*This house smaller than that one.*
Esa señora es más importante que este señor.	*That lady is more important than this gentleman.*
Juanito es menor que Dinita.	*Juanito is younger than Dinita.*
Gloria es mayor que Lili.	*Gloria is older than Lili.*
México D.F. es la ciudad más grande del mundo.	*Mexico City is the largest city in the world.*

 ◄ **8.11** ►

DIALOG 2
Vamos a las pirámides · *Let's go to the pyramids*

David and Anita make plans to visit the ruins of the holy city of Teotihuacán. They are going to the travel agency counter next to the reception desk.

David y Anita hacen planes para visitar las ruinas de la ciudad sagrada de Teotihuacán.

ANITA   David, ¿no te gustaría ir a Teotihuacán mañana?

DAVID   ¡Claro! ¡Me encantaría ir! Vamos a la recepción del hotel. Allí hay un mostrador de una agencia de viajes que tiene anuncios de viajes por el día.

(Los dos esposos van a la agencia y hablan con la agente de viajes.)

ANITA   Señorita, quisiéramos información sobre una gira para visitar las pirámides de Teotihuacán.

AGENTE   Tenemos una gira que sale cada mañana desde aquí. Un autobús viene a recogerlos a las nueve en punto y los trae de vuelta a las cuatro de la tarde.

DAVID   ¿Qué incluye el precio de la gira?

AGENTE   Incluye primero una visita a Acolmán para ver la iglesia de los Agustinos. Es una iglesia gótica muy antigua y hermosa que data de 1539. Luego, el viaje continúa hasta Teotihuacán, donde pueden subir a las pirámides del Sol y de la Luna y visitar el templo de Quetzalcoatl. En el viaje de vuelta hay una visita a la Basílica de Guadalupe, la patrona de México.

ANITA   ¡Fantástico! ¡Vamos a estar aquí mañana a las nueve en punto!

◄ 8.12 ►
Vocabulario

hacen planes	*they make plans*
la ciudad sagrada	*holy city*
allí	*there*
el mostrador	*counter*
la agencia de viajes	*travel agency*
la gira	*tour*
sale (salir) (*irregular*)	*it leaves, it departs*
cada	*each, every*
aquí	*here*
recogerlos	*to pick you up*
en punto	*on the dot*
los trae de vuelta	*it brings you back*
incluye (incluir)	*it includes*
el precio	*price*
la iglesia	*church*
gótico(-a)	*Gothic*
data de	*it dates to*
subir	*to go up, to climb*
la pirámide	*pyramid*
el sol	*sun*
la luna	*moon*
en el viaje de vuelta	*on the way back*
una visita	*a visit*

Expresión idiomática

When we want to emphasize the fact that we should be punctual, we use the expression **en punto** ("on the dot").

◄ **8.13** ►
Estructura gramatical

More irregular verbs

Irregular verbs are verbs that change the ending and the stem, usually without a pattern. Some important irregular verbs are **dar**, **hacer**, **salir**, **venir**, and **valer**.

DAR ("to give")	HACER ("to do, make")	SALIR ("to go out")
doy	hago	salgo
das	haces	sales
da	hace	sale
damos	hacemos	salimos
dan	hacen	salen

VENIR ("to come")	VALER ("to be worth")
vengo	valgo
vienes	vales
viene	vale
venimos	valemos
vienen	valen

The verbs **ser** and **estar**

SER	ESTAR
soy	estoy
eres	estás
es	está
somos	estamos
son	están

Ser answers the question "What?"

¡**Qué** eres?
Soy americano, católico, republicano, profesor.

¡**Cómo** eres?
Soy alto, gordo, inteligente. (*characteristics*)

Estar answers the questions "How?" and "Where?"

> **¿Cómo estás?**
> **Estoy** bien, contento, sentado. (*conditions*)
>
> **¿Dónde estás?**
> **Estoy** en Madrid, en mi casa. (*locations*)

◄ **8.14** ►
Audio practice

The irregular verb ir

As we have seen, not all Spanish verbs change just the ending. Some verbs, called irregular verbs, change the ending and the stem, or sometimes the whole word changes. For instance, the verb **ir** ("to go") changes to **voy, vas, va, vamos, van.**

Notice the use of irregular verbs in the following conversation.

MARÍA	Eduardo, ¿adónde vas?
EDUARDO	Voy a casa de Juan. Tengo que darle este libro. ¿Vienes conmigo?
MARÍA	Me gustaría ir, pero en este momento hago algo muy importante, ¡compro zapatos! Manolo da una fiesta mañana.
EDUARDO	¡Ah! Yo también voy a esa fiesta. Las fiestas de Manolo valen un Perú.

Listen to the recording to practice the following exchanges.

¿Qué haces?	*What are you doing?*
Hago ejercicio.	*I am exercising.*
¿Adónde vas?	*Where are you going?*
Voy al supermercado.	*I am going to the supermarket.*
¿Cuánto valen esos zapatos?	*How much do those shoes cost?*
Valen $80.	*They cost $80.*
¿Qué le das a Gabriel?	*What are you giving Gabriel?*
Le doy unas entradas para el ballet.	*I am giving him some tickets for the ballet.*
¿A qué hora sales?	*What time are you leaving?*
Salgo a las cuatro de la tarde.	*I am leaving at 4 P.M.*

¿Cuándo vienen Uds.?	*When are you coming?*
Venimos mañana.	*We are coming tomorrow.*
¿Con quién vienes?	*Whom are you coming with?*
Vengo con María.	*I am coming with María.*
¿Qué hacen Uds.?	*What are you doing?*
Nosotros salimos al patio.	*We are going out onto the patio.*

◄ 8.15 ►
Exercise

Complete the following questions with the correct form of the verb in parentheses.

1. Catalina y su mamá _____ al cine a ver *Gladiador*. (ir)

2. Yo _____ mi trabajo rápidamente. (hacer)

3. Tú _____ con nosotros. (venir)

4. Esos zapatos _____ mucho dinero, ¡300 dólares! (valer)

5. Nosotros _____ dinero a los pobres. (dar)

6. Ellos _____ mucho trabajo. (tener)

7. Yo _____ a las ocho de la mañana. (salir)

8. Ellos _____ ejercicio en el gimnasio. (hacer)

9. Yo le _____ un libro al estudiante. (dar)

◄ 8.16 ►
Audio practice

Ser and estar

As we have seen, Spanish has two verbs to express the English verb "to be." If we are talking about a characteristic or identifying someone or something, then we use **ser**. For instance, the travel agent tells our friends that the church of the Agustines **es una iglesia gótica** because she is talking about a characteristic of the church. When we are telling where someone or something is or expressing a temporary condition, we use **estar**. For instance, Anita tells the travel agent **Vamos a estar aquí mañana a las nueve en punto.**

Look at the following dialog and see if you understand clearly why they are using two different verbs to express "to be." David is asking a gentleman about a popular restaurant, and the gentleman gives information about the characteristics of the restaurant and its location.

DAVID   Señor, ¿dónde está el restaurante Focolare?

SEÑOR   Está en la calle Hamburgo, en la Zona Rosa.

DAVID   ¿Es un restaurante típico?

SEÑOR   Sí, es muy bonito y es muy popular.

DAVID   Muchas gracias por la información. Anita, ¿estás cansada? (cansada, *tired*)

ANITA   Estoy un poco cansada, pero estoy entusiasmada con la idea de comer allí.

Now David and Anita are in the restaurant talking about the food.

DAVID   ¡Este huachinango está delicioso! (huachinango, *red snapper*)

ANITA   ¿Es un plato picante? (picante, *spicy*)

DAVID   No es picante; otros platos son picantes. ¿Cómo están tus camarones?

ANITA   Están deliciosos, pero es un plato muy grande. ¡Voy a comer hasta mañana!

DAVID   Estoy muy contento de estar aquí.

◄ 8.17 ►
Exercise

Complete the following sentences with the correct form of **ser** or **estar**.

1. La Casa Blanca _____ en Washington.

2. Estos camarones _____ deliciosos.

3. Tu amigo Federico _____ muy inteligente.

4. Mi coche _____ viejo. ¡_____ de 1985!

5. Nosotros _____ cansados.

6. Ellos _____ entusiasmados.

7. El Museo del Prado _____ en Madrid.

8. El Museo Antropológico de México D.F. _____ muy famoso.

9. Frida Kahlo y Diego Rivera _____ artistas famosos.

 ◄ **8.18** ►
DIALOG 3
Descansando en Acapulco · *Resting in Acapulco*

After their visit to Mexico City and its surroundings, Anita and David go to Acapulco to rest for a couple of days. They choose a hotel in the Costera Miguel Alemán (a main thoroughfare) because they want to be close to the beach. There they rest, sunbathe, and swim, enjoying the beautiful sea. That night they make plans to go to the old part of the city the next morning, and afterwards to see the brave divers who dive from La Quebrada every day.

Después de visitar la ciudad de México y los alrededores, David y Anita van a Acapulco para descansar un par de días. Escogen un hotel en la Costera Miguel Alemán porque quieren estar cerca de la playa. Allí descansan, toman el sol y nadan, disfrutando del hermoso mar. Esa noche hacen planes para ir a la parte vieja de la ciudad a la mañana siguiente, y después ir a ver a los valientes clavadistas que se lanzan desde La Quebrada cada día.

ANITA Me gustaría ir a la parte antigua de la ciudad para visitar el Mercado Municipal. Allí venden objetos típicos de cerámica. Quisiera comprar unos recuerdos y al mismo tiempo tener la oportunidad de regatear. Allí también podemos visitar la iglesia y el Fuerte San Diego.

DAVID ¿Sabes? También quisiera ver a los clavadistas en La Quebrada.

ANITA Pues, La Quebrada no está muy lejos. Podemos ir primero al Viejo Acapulco y después a La Quebrada. Dicen que los clavadistas son extraordinarios. No sé cómo pueden lanzarse desde tanta altura.

DAVID Pues, ¡son muy machos!

◄ **8.19** ►
Vocabulario

los alrededores	*surroundings*
descansar	*to rest*

un par	*a pair, a couple*
escogen (escoger)	*they choose*
cerca	*near*
la playa	*beach*
toman el sol	*they sunbathe*
nadan	*they swim*
disfrutando (disfrutar)	*enjoying*
el hermoso mar	*beautiful sea*
viejo(-a)	*old, worn out*
los/las clavadistas	*cliff divers*
la mañana siguiente	*the next morning*
antiguo(-a)	*old, ancient, from another era*
los recuerdos	*souvenirs*
regatear	*to bargain*
dicen (decir) (*irregular*)	*they say*
lanzarse	*to dive, to fling oneself*
tanta altura	*so much height*

Vocabulario adicional

lejos	*far*
esquiar en el agua	*to water ski*
el esquí acuático	*waterskiing*
pasear en velero	*to go sailing*
pasear en bote	*to go for a boat ride*
bucear	*to snorkel*
ir de pesca	*to go fishing*
remar	*to row*

◄ **8.20** ►
Estructura gramatical

Other common irregular verbs

SABER ("to know")	CONOCER ("to know")	DECIR ("to say")	TRAER ("to bring")
sé	conozco	digo	traigo
sabes	conoces	dices	traes
sabe	conoce	dice	trae
sabemos	conocemos	decimos	traemos
saben	conocen	dicen	traen

CAER	OÍR	PONER
("to fall")	("to hear")	("to put")
caigo	oigo	pongo
caes	oyes	pones
cae	oye	pone
caemos	oímos	ponemos
caen	oyen	ponen

There are two verbs meaning "to know." **Saber** means to know information, and **conocer** means to know places or people.

Sé tu número de teléfono.	*I know your telephone number.*
Sabemos hablar inglés.	*We know how to speak English.*
Conozco Madrid.	*I know Madrid.*
¿Conoces a Carlos González?	*Do you know Carlos González?*

Noun + adjective

The noun is generally placed before the adjective. For instance, Anita says that she would like to go to **la parte antigua de la ciudad**. Remember that the adjective must agree in gender and number with the noun.

Nevertheless, sometimes for emphasis the adjective is placed before the noun, like when David talks about **el Viejo Acapulco**. This also happens with possessive, demonstrative, and numerical adjectives: *mi* **casa**, *estos* **camarones**, *tres* **playas**.

With adjectives such as **bueno** and **malo**, the adjective changes slightly.

un amigo **bueno**	un **buen** amigo
un amigo **malo**	un **mal** amigo

We may place these adjectives before the noun for emphasis.

With adjectives such as **grande**, **pobre**, **nuevo**, and **viejo**, changing the position changes the meaning.

¡Pobre hombre!	*Poor man! (we feel sorry for him)*
Fernando es un hombre pobre.	*Fernando is a poor man.*
	(he doesn't have money)

Lincoln fue un gran hombre.	*Lincoln was a great man.*
Lincoln fue un hombre grande.	*Lincoln was a big man.*
Compré el nuevo auto.	*I bought the latest model.*
Compré un auto nuevo.	*I bought a new car.*
Tengo un amigo viejo.	*I have a friend who is old.*
Tengo un viejo amigo.	*I have an old friend. (he has been my friend for years)*

Comprensión y expresión

Let's review the irregular verb **saber**.

sé
sabes
sabe
sabemos
saben

On the recording you will hear David use this verb in the following conversation. He is talking to Anita about bargaining, a common practice in Spanish-speaking countries.

DAVID ¿Sabes regatear? No lo hacemos en los Estados Unidos.
ANITA Tú sabes que vivimos un año en Sudamérica, por eso sé hacerlo.
DAVID Entonces, tu mamá sabe regatear muy bien.
ANITA Mi mamá y yo sabemos regatear perfectamente.

Saber means to know information. However, if we want to say that we know places or people, we must use the verb **conocer**. Repeat these forms.

conozco
conoces
conoce
conocemos
conocen

This verb is used in the following conversation on the recording.

DAVID   ¿Conoces la ciudad de Guadalajara?

ANITA   Sí, la conozco. Allí conozco a dos mexicanos muy simpáticos.

DAVID   ¿Los conozco?

ANITA   Conoces a uno. Conoces a Raúl, pero no te preocupes.
      Ellos te conocen.

Other irregular verbs that we first encountered on pages 123–124 are **decir**, **caer**, **traer**, and **oír**. These verbs all have a **g** in the first person (**digo**, **caigo**, **traigo**, **oigo**). In addition, **decir** has other changes in its stem (**digo**, **dices**, **dice**, **decimos**, **dicen**), as does **oír** (**oigo**, **oyes**, **oye**, **oímos**, **oyen**).

These verbs are used in the following conversation between Carlos and María, where María says that she falls when she climbs on a chair. Luckily, Carlos has his radio and the two can listen to Mexican music, which makes María happy.

CARLOS   Me dicen que te caes cada vez que te subes a una silla.

MARÍA   Sí, me caigo porque tengo vértigo. ¿Traes tu radio contigo?

CARLOS   Sí, la traigo y oigo unos mariachis.

MARÍA   ¿Me permites oír? Cuando oigo música mexicana me pongo
      contenta. (ponerse, *to become*)

◄ 8.22 ►
Exercise

Complete the following sentences with the correct form of the verb in parentheses.

1. Yo no _____ hablar ruso. (saber)

2. Ellos _____ música clásica. (oír)

3. Nosotros _____ que estos camarones están
   deliciosos. (decir)

4. Tú _____ las bebidas para el picnic. (traer)

5. Ud. _____ el sombrero en la silla. (poner)

6. Yo _____ los platos. (traer)

7. Yo no me _____ de la silla. (caer)

8. Ella no _____ cómo me llamo. (saber)

9. Yo no _____ Nepal. (conocer)

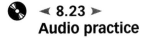 ◄ **8.23** ►
Audio practice

Bargaining is done throughout Latin America. Listen to Anita bargaining with a Mexican vendor at the market, then repeat.

ANITA	Quisiera ver esa blusa bordada. (blusa bordada, *embroidered blouse*)
VENDEDOR	¿Esta blusa roja? (rojo[-a], *red*)
ANITA	No, esa blusa blanca. ¿Cuánto vale? (blanco[-a], *white*) (¿Cuánto vale? *How much does it cost?*)
VENDEDOR	Vale 250 pesos.
ANITA	¡Es muy cara! La llevo por 100 pesos. (caro[-a], *expensive*)
VENDEDOR	¡Señora, es imposible! El mejor precio que puedo darle es 200 pesos.
ANITA	Le doy 150 pesos. No puedo pagar más.
VENDEDOR	Está bien, por ser para Ud., se la doy por 150 pesos. (por ser para Ud., *because it is for you*)

Anita is planning more shopping in the following conversation. Notice her use of adjectives.

ANITA	Me gusta mucho ese sarape rojo y no es caro. ¿Te gusta?
DAVID	Sí, pero me gustaría comprar esta pulsera de plata para ti. (pulsera de plata, *silver bracelet*)
ANITA	Las cosas de plata son muy caras.
DAVID	Pero tú eres una fantástica regatona, entonces puedes pedir un precio mejor. (regatona, *haggler*)
ANITA	Sí, regateo bien, pero no soy una buena perdedora. Si el vendedor no me da el precio que quiero, no la vamos a comprar.
DAVID	Estoy seguro de que la vamos a comprar.

Notice that Anita says **regateo bien** ("I bargain well") but **buena perdedora** ("good loser"). **Bien** (adverb) and **bueno(-a)** (adjective) are sometimes confusing. Don't forget that **bien** goes with a verb!

◄ 8.24 ►
Exercise

¿Cómo se dice en español? These are some of the expressions used in this chapter. Write the Spanish equivalent.

1. a good car   _____

2. a bad loser   _____

3. some expensive shoes   _____

4. the best price   _____

5. a white blouse   _____

6. an old vendor
    (he is an old man)   _____

◄ 8.25 ►
Expresión libre

Using what you have learned in this chapter, answer the speaker in a spontaneous conversation about traveling.

◄ 8.26 ►
¡Viva la diferencia!

• Mexico D.F. is the largest city in the world, with 20 million inhabitants. It is a bustling metropolis, full of interesting historic and artistic places to visit. **El Palacio de Bellas Artes**, the fine arts theater, is a beautiful marble building where the **Ballet Folklórico de México** performs their spectacular rendition of Mexican regional folk dances. Two performances are given every Sunday and Wednesday. **La Zona Rosa** is an elegant downtown section of cafés, restaurants, hotels, galleries, and stores. Chapultepec Castle was the residence of Emperor Maximiliano and several presidents until it was converted to the National History Museum in 1940. Frida Kahlo's house is a bright blue adobe house where the painter was born and lived with her husband, Diego Rivera.

• Teotihuacán is an ancient sacred city whose relics were discovered by the Aztecs. The Pyramid of the Sun, with 248 steps to climb, and the Pyramid of the Moon are the two main pyramids. Another impressive building is the Temple of Quetzalcoatl, a god who taught the Aztecs about life and fertility, then sailed east, promising to return. He is represented as a plumed serpent. The entire city encompasses eight square miles. The artifacts uncovered at this site can be seen at the **Museo Antropológico** in Mexico City.

• The Virgin of Guadalupe is the patron saint of the Mexican nation. There are in fact two Basilicas of the Virgin of Guadalupe. The Old Basilica dates to 1536. It is believed that on December 12, 1531, the Virgin gave an Indian boy, Juan Diego, a cloth with an imprint of her image. The New Basilica was built in 1976 when the old church could no longer be used.

• Acapulco is a popular resort on the Pacific coast, 175 miles south of Mexico City. The Costera Miguel Alemán is a wide boulevard that encircles Acapulco Bay. Many hotels, malls, restaurants, and night clubs are located on the Costera. At La Quebrada, a cliff 130 feet high, divers plunge every day into the surf.

• A **mariachi** is either a group of musicians playing Mexican music, or one of the musicians in the band.

◄ **8.27** ►
How to make it sound Spanish

Be careful when you pronounce words like **cada** ("each"), **todo** ("everything"), and **lodo** ("mud"). The tendency is to pronounce them the English way: /kada/, /todo/, /lodo/. But if you do so, you are saying **cara** ("face"), **toro** ("bull"), and **loro** ("parrot"), which is not what you want to say. Pronounce the **d** between vowels like /th/, as in English "this": /katha/, /totho/, /lotho/!

◄ 9 ►

Lo pasamos muy bien
We had a great time

OBJECTIVE

In this chapter you will learn how to express something that happened in the past, how to talk about weather conditions in the present and in the past, and how to say how long ago something happened or has been happening. You will also become acquainted with two common verbs, "to have a good (or bad) time" and "to realize," and you will learn the expression "speaking about _____."

9.1

DIALOG 1
¡Fuimos a Oaxaca! · *We went to Oaxaca!*

Anita and David have traveled to Oaxaca. That night, after seeing the city, they talk in the hotel garden while they have a cold drink. When they visited the Santo Domingo Church, an extraordinary example of Baroque style, they saw an exhibition in the convent next to the church; they also admired fine examples of pre-Columbian art at the Rufino Tamayo Museum of Pre-Hispanic Art. Their tour to the ruins of Monte Albán the next day will give them the chance to see how the ancient people, the Zapotecas, lived. At the convent exhibition they have already seen the treasure of gold and jade jewelry found in one of the tombs of what was once a city of 40,000 people.

Anita y David viajaron a Oaxaca esa mañana, donde se hospedaron en el Hotel Casa Carreño. Esa noche, después de visitar la ciudad, hablan en el jardín del hotel mientras beben un refresco.

ANITA   Oaxaca es un tesoro colonial. De todas las iglesias que visitamos hoy, ¡y en Oaxaca hay muchas!, la más fantástica es la iglesia de Santo Domingo. No es posible ver en una sola visita todo el arte que decora las paredes y el techo.

DAVID   Sí, nunca antes vi una iglesia barroca tan hermosa. Y la exposición histórica y artística que hay en el convento es realmente importante. También me gustó mucho el Museo de Arte Prehispánico de Rufino Tamayo. Es una colección impresionante de arte precolombino.

ANITA   A propósito de arte precolombino, tenemos billetes para la gira a Monte Albán mañana a las nueve de la mañana. Estoy muy contenta de poder visitar esas ruinas. Quiero ver cómo vivieron 40.000 zapotecas en esa gran ciudad. Leí que cuando abrieron una de las tumbas, encontraron un tesoro incalculable de joyas de oro, jade, perlas y marfil.

DAVID   Claro, las joyas que vimos en el Museo Regional en el convento de Santo Domingo son parte de ese tesoro.

◄ 9.2 ►
Vocabulario

se hospedaron (hospedarse)	*they stayed overnight*
el jardín	*garden*
el tesoro	*treasure*
la iglesia	*church*
barroca	*Baroque*
la exposición	*exhibition*
el arte	*art*
a propósito	*by the way*
a propósito de _____	*speaking of _____*
contento(-a)	*happy*
las ruinas	*ruins*
leí (leer)	*I read*
abrieron (abrir)	*they opened*
la tumba	*tomb*
encontraron (encontrar) (o>ue)	*they found*
el oro	*gold*
las perlas	*pearls*
el marfil	*ivory*
vimos (ver) (*irregular*)	*we saw*
el convento	*convent*
la parte	*part*

Expresiones idiomáticas

Anita says **a propósito de Monte Albán**, meaning "speaking of Monte Albán." This expression can also be used to mean "by the way," followed by a comma; in this case we just say **a propósito**. For example, we can say, **A propósito, tengo un libro excelente sobre Monte Albán** ("By the way, I have an excellent book about Monte Albán"), or **A propósito de Monte Albán, estuve allí el año pasado** ("Speaking of Monte Albán, I was there last year").

The title of this chapter is **We had a great time**. For a person who is not a native Spanish speaker, the tendency is to say **tuvimos buen tiempo**, which actually means "we had good weather." The correct way to express this phrase in Spanish is to say **lo pasamos muy bien** or **nos divertimos mucho**. The next time someone asks you **¿Cómo lo pasaste?** ("Did you have a good time?"), you should answer **Lo pasé (muy) bien**. You have to use **lo** and the preterite tense of **pasar** (**lo pasé, lo pasaste, lo pasó, lo pasamos, lo pasaron**) and then **bien** or **muy bien**.

◄ **9.3** ►
Estructura gramatical
Preterite of regular verbs

David says **Nunca antes vi una iglesia...** ("I never before saw a church . . ."), and later in the dialog Anita says **quiero ver cómo vivieron...** ("I want to see how they lived . . ."). They are using the past tense called **pretérito** in Spanish. This is the tense used to express definite actions in the past. The preterite is the tense that expresses what happened—always a definite and complete action in the past.

> Abrí la ventana dos veces.   *I opened the window twice.*

When we want to describe something in the past, or when the action is not definite, we use another tense.

Preterite tense endings for regular verbs are different from present tense endings. If a regular verb ends in **-ar**, the endings are **-é, -aste, -ó, -amos, -aron**. If a regular verb ends in **-er** or **–ir**, the endings are **-í, -iste, -ió, -imos, -ieron**.

Notice how Anita uses the preterite in these statements.

> **Encontraron** un tesoro...   *They found a treasure . . .*
> **Leí** que cuando **abrieron**...   *I read that when they opened . . .*

Here are the preterite forms for the regular -**ar** verbs **viajar** and **hablar**.

VIAJAR ("to travel")	HABLAR ("to speak")
viajé	hablé
viajaste	hablaste
viajó	habló
viajamos	hablamos
viajaron	hablaron

All -**ar** verbs are conjugated the same way in the preterite.

Here are the preterite forms for the -er and -ir verbs **comer**, **abrir**, and **leer**. Notice that **leer** changes the **i** to **y** in the third-person preterite forms.

COMER ("to eat")	ABRIR ("to open")	LEER ("to read")
comí	abrí	leí
comiste	abriste	leíste
comió	abrió	leyó
comimos	abrimos	leímos
comieron	abrieron	leyeron

Ayer ("yesterday") and **anoche** ("last night") become important words when we use the preterite. **La semana pasada** ("last week"), **el año pasado** ("last year"), **el lunes/martes pasado** ("last Monday/Tuesday") are also frequent expressions.

◄ 9.4 ►
Audio practice

In this conversation, Anita and David are talking about the things they saw at Monte Albán and what happened to them at a rug factory.

ANITA   ¿Qué te gustó más de Monte Albán?

DAVID   Me gustó todo.

ANITA   Vi que tomaste muchas fotos.

DAVID   Anita, ¿por qué no compraste esa figurita de jade que te ofrecieron?

ANITA   Porque pensé que en el mercado de Oaxaca la vi a un precio más barato. (barato, *inexpensive*).

DAVID   Sí, también vi alfombras más baratas en Oaxaca.

ANITA   El dueño de la fábrica se enojó porque no compramos la alfombra que nos ofreció. (el dueño, *owner*; la fábrica, *factory*; se enojó, *got mad*)

DAVID   El año pasado compré una alfombra por la mitad del precio. (la mitad, *half*)

ANITA   Pero el año pasado no comiste tan bien como comimos ayer.

David is quite definite when he says **Me gustó todo**. He also says that he took many pictures and asks Anita why she did not buy the jade figurine. Finally, at the end of the dialog David says that he bought a rug last year and Anita says that they ate very well yesterday. As you can see, they are talking about definite actions, so they use the preterite.

On the recording you will hear the following exchanges using the preterite tense.

¿Te gustó?	*Did you like it?*
Sí, me gustó.	*Yes, I liked it.*
¿Viste la película?	*Did you see the movie?*
Sí, vi la película.	*Yes, I saw the movie.*
¿Tomaste muchas fotos?	*Did you take many photos?*
Sí, tomé muchas fotos.	*Yes, I took many photos.*
¿Compraste la figurita?	*Did you buy the figurine?*
No, no la compré.	*No, I did not buy it.*
¿Te ofrecieron ayuda?	*Did they offer you help?*
Sí, me ofrecieron ayuda.	*Yes, they offered me help.*
¿Pediste la ensalada?	*Did you ask for a salad?*
No, pedí la sopa de pollo.	*No, I asked for chicken soup.*
¿Se enojó el dueño?	*Did the owner get mad?*
Sí, el dueño se enojó.	*Yes, the owner got mad.*
¿Comiste bien?	*Did you eat well?*
Sí, comí muy bien.	*Yes, I ate very well.*

◄ **9.5** ►
Exercise

Complete the following sentences with the correct preterite tense form of the verb in parentheses.

1. La agente de viaje nos _____ a preparar la gira. (ayudar) (ayudar, *to help*)

2. Carolina _____ una alfombra muy barata. (comprar)

3. Yo _____ contigo ayer por la mañana. (hablar)

4. Nosotros _____ en esa universidad el verano pasado. (estudiar)

5. Tú _____ el piso ayer. (limpiar)

6. Ellos _____ en el concierto del martes pasado. (cantar) (cantar, *to sing*)

7. ¿Le _____ a Ud. esa ciudad? (gustar)

8. Uds. _____ a muchas personas. (invitar)

9. Ellos lo _____ muy bien en la fiesta. (pasar)

◄ 9.6 ►
Audio practice

In the following conversation, José and his sister Alicia use the preterite constantly. Listen to the recording and practice by pausing to repeat.

JOSÉ	¿Comiste ya? (ya, *already*)
ALICIA	Sí, ya comí.
JOSÉ	¿Qué bebiste?
ALICIA	Bebí limonada.
JOSÉ	¿Leíste la noticia del accidente?
ALICIA	Sí, la leí. ¡Qué terrible!
JOSÉ	¿Saliste esta mañana?
ALICIA	Sí, salí.
JOSÉ	¿Compraste las fresas para el postre?
ALICIA	Sí, las compré.
JOSÉ	¿Llamaste a Tinito por teléfono?
ALICIA	No, olvidé llamarlo, pero ahora lo llamo.

◄ 9.7 ►
Exercise

Complete the following sentences with the correct preterite tense form of the verb in parentheses.

1. Carmen _____ una carta a su familia ayer. (escribir)

2. Marta y Raquel _____ en un restaurante mexicano anoche. (comer)

3. Yo no _____ con Ricardo la semana pasada. (hablar)

4. Nosotros _____ dos años en Madrid. (vivir)

5. Ud. _____ muy bien el problema. (explicar)

6. Tú _____ esa puerta, ¿verdad? (abrir)

7. Yo _____ unos tomates muy baratos. (comprar)

8. ¿_____ tú la nueva revista? (leer)

9. Ellos no _____ la explicación. (comprender)

10. Ud. _____ la puerta. (abrir)

 ◄ 9.8 ►
DIALOG 2
Nos perdimos, pero... · *We got lost, but . . .*

Anita and David are in Yucatán; they arrived three days ago in Mérida. They visited the city first, and yesterday they went to Chichén Itzá. This morning, while having breakfast, they remember the places they visited during those two days, and how they got lost in Chichén Itzá.

Anita y David están en Yucatán. Llegaron hace tres días a Mérida. Primero visitaron la ciudad y ayer fueron a Chichén Itzá. Esta mañana mientras toman desayuno, recuerdan los lugares que visitaron durante esos dos días.

ANITA   Mérida es una ciudad muy interesante.

DAVID   ¿Sabes? El zócalo fue el centro de la antigua ciudad maya.

ANITA   Creo que lo más impresionante que vi hasta ahora en este viaje fue Chichén Itzá. Los mayas y toltecas tuvieron un centro religioso espectacular.

DAVID   Lo único que no me gustó es que nos perdimos. ¿Cómo nos separamos del grupo?

ANITA   No me di cuenta. Sólo sé que caminamos muchísimo hasta que no vimos más la ciudad.

DAVID   Por suerte encontramos a esos dos mexicanos tan amables que caminaron con nosotros hasta que encontramos a nuestro grupo.

ANITA   Sí, fueron extremadamente amables. Tuvimos mucha suerte.

DAVID   Sí, también tuvimos suerte que no hizo el calor que dicen que va a hacer hoy.

◄ 9.9 ►
Vocabulario´

hace tres días	*three days ago*
fueron (ir) (*irregular*)	*they went*
fue el centro	*it was the center*

vi (ver) (*irregular*)	*I saw*
tuvieron (tener) (*irregular*)	*they had*
lo único	*the only thing*
nos perdimos (perderse) (e>ie)	*we got lost*
nos separamos (separarse)	*we got separated*
no me di cuenta	*I did not realize*
sólo	*only*
no vimos más	*we no longer saw*
por suerte	*luckily*
tan amables	*so nice*
hasta que	*until*
tuvimos suerte	*we were lucky*
no hizo el calor	*it was not as hot*
va a hacer hoy	*is going to be today*

Expresión idiomática

When David says that he did not realize how they got separated from the group, he says **no me di cuenta**. The verb is **darse cuenta de**. There is a verb **realizar**, but it means "to accomplish." Therefore, when you want to say "he accomplished his dream," you say **él realizó su sueño**, but when you want to say "he did not realize the time," you must say **no se dio cuenta de la hora**.

 ◄ **9.10** ►
Estructura gramatical

Irregular preterite tense verbs

David says **el zócalo fue el centro de la antigua ciudad maya**. He is saying that the **zócalo** ("plaza") was the center of the old Mayan city. The verbs **ser** and **ir** actually share the same forms in the preterite tense.

SER ("to be") and IR ("to go")

fui
fuiste
fue
fuimos
fueron

Fui a México.	*I went to Mexico.*
Fui su amigo.	*I was his friend.*

Here are other irregular preterites.

ESTAR ("to be")	TENER ("to have")
estuve	tuve
estuviste	tuviste
estuvo	tuvo
estuvimos	tuvimos
estuvieron	tuvieron

DECIR ("to say")	DAR ("to give")
dije	di
dijiste	diste
dijo	dio
dijimos	dimos
dijeron	dieron

Practice the following sentences on the recording.

Ellos fueron a Portugal.	*They went to Portugal.*
Tú no fuiste al gimnasio ayer.	*You didn't go to the gym yesterday.*
Nosotras fuimos amigas.	*We were friends.*
Uds. fueron candidatos.	*You were candidates.*
Tú fuiste la mejor.	*You were the best.*
Yo fui a casa a las seis.	*I went home at six.*

◄ 9.11 ►

Comprensión y expresión

Describing the weather

David says **no hizo calor** ("it was not hot") the day they got lost in Chichén Itzá. We use the verb **hacer** when we want to express weather conditions. The question is **¿Qué tiempo hace hoy?** for the present and **¿Qué tiempo hizo _____?** for the preterite.

Hace mucho (poco) calor (frío, fresco).	*It is very (a little) hot (cold, cool).*
Hace poco calor hoy.	*It is just a little hot today. (It is not very hot.)*
Hizo mucho frío el invierno pasado.	*It was very cold last winter.*
Hace viento en el otoño.	*It is windy in the fall.*
Hizo sol ayer.	*It was sunny yesterday.*

Hace buen tiempo hoy.   *The weather is good today.*
Hizo fresco el jueves   *It was cool last Thursday.*
    pasado.

Practice the following exchanges on the recording.

¿Qué tiempo hace hoy?
What is the weather like today?

Hoy hace frío.
It is cold today.

¿Qué tiempo hace esta tarde?
What is the weather like this afternoon?

Hace viento, pero hace buen tiempo.
It's windy, but good weather.

¿Qué tiempo hizo ayer?
What was the weather like yesterday?

Ayer hizo sol y mucho calor.
Yesterday it was sunny and very hot.

¿Qué tiempo hizo la semana pasada?
What was the weather like last week?

La semana pasada hizo fresco.
Last week it was cool.

Saying how long ago

Hacer is also used when we want to express the idea of "how long ago." For instance, when we want to say that Anita and David arrived in Mérida three days ago, we say **llegaron hace tres días.**

To express "how long ago," we use **hace** + length of time + **que** + verb. Be careful to not use the preterite form of **hacer.**

Hace dos días que estamos aquí.	*We have been here for two days.*
Ellos comieron allí hace tres días.	*They ate there three days ago.*

Practice the following exchanges on the recording.

¿Hace cuántos días que estás aquí?	*How many days have you been here?*
Hace diez días que estoy aquí.	*I've been here for ten days.*
¿Hace cuántos años que ellos viven en Santiago?	*How many years have they lived in Santiago?*
Hace ocho años que viven en Santiago.	*They've lived in Santiago for eight years.*
¿Hace cuánto tiempo que Uds. viajaron a Tucumán?	*How long ago did you travel to Tucumán?*
Hace un año y medio que viajamos a Tucumán.	*We traveled to Tucumán one and a half years ago.*
¿Hace cuánto tiempo que hablaste con Ricardo?	*How long has it been since you spoke with Ricardo?*
Hace un mes que hablé con él.	*It's been a month since I spoke with him.*
¿Hace cuántas horas que fuiste al mercado?	*How many hours ago did you go to the market?*
Hace tres horas que fui al mercado.	*I went to the market three hours ago.*

◄ 9.12 ►
Audio practice

Irregular preterite

Some verbs have irregular preterite forms. For instance, the preterite of **ser** is **fui, fuiste, fue, fuimos, fueron**. The verb **ir** has the same preterite forms. **Dar, estar, tener,** and **decir** are also irregular in the preterite. On the recording, practice the following examples.

¿Fuiste a Puerto Vallarta?	*Did you go to Puerto Vallarta?*
No, fui a Acapulco.	*No, I went to Acapulco.*
¿Fueron amigos Uds.?	*Were you friends?*
Sí, fuimos amigos.	*Yes, we were friends.*
¿Fue Ud. al cine anoche?	*Did you go to the movies last night?*
No, fui al teatro.	*No, I went to the theater.*
¿Me diste los billetes?	*Did you give me the tickets?*
Sí, te di los billetes.	*Yes, I gave you the tickets.*
¿Nos dieron Uds. la llave?	*Did you give us the key?*
Sí, les dimos la llave.	*Yes, we gave you the key.*
¿Estuviste en Puerto Rico el año pasado?	*Were you in Puerto Rico last year?*
No, estuve en la República Dominicana.	*No, I was in the Dominican Republic.*
¿Tuvieron problemas Uds.?	*Did you have any problems?*
No, no tuvimos problemas.	*No, we didn't have any problems.*
¿Le dijiste a Elena?	*Did you tell Elena?*
Sí, le dije a Elena.	*Yes, I told Elena.*

◄ 9.13 ►
Audio practice

Anita and David are talking about the tour they took today. On the recording, listen to the irregular preterites they use, especially their use of **hacer**. The verb **hacer** means "to do" or "to make," but it is also used to express weather conditions such as **hace frío** ("it is cold") or **hizo frío** ("it was cold"), **hace sol** ("it is sunny") or **hizo sol** ("it was sunny"), etc. Listen and then repeat after the pause.

ANITA   ¡Hizo mucho calor hoy!

DAVID   Hizo más calor que ayer, pero hizo viento.

ANITA   ¿Qué dijo el guía sobre la semana pasada?

DAVID   Dijo que hizo fresco, y no hizo sol en toda la semana.

ANITA   Ese guía fue muy amable. ¿Le diste una buena propina?

DAVID   Sí, fui generoso porque fue amable y dio explicaciones claras.

◄ 9.14 ►
Exercise

Complete the following sentences with the correct preterite form of the verb in parentheses.

1. Elena y Carlos nos _____ un postre delicioso. (dar)

2. La señora Estévez _____ un problema. (tener)

3. Ud. no me _____ que viajó la semana pasada. (decir)

4. Nosotros _____ que hacer mucho ejercicio. (tener)

5. Ayer _____ mucho calor. (hacer)

6. Yo le _____ una buena propina al camarero. (dar)

7. ¿Me _____ (tú) la cámara? (dar)

8. ¿_____ Ud. presidente de esa compañía? (ser)

9. Mis amigos _____ a Acapulco el verano pasado. (ir)

10. ¿Cuántos días _____ Uds. en Oaxaca? (estar)

11. Simón Bolívar _____ un hombre extraordinario. (ser)

◄ 9.15 ►
Audio practice

The verb **hacer** is also used to express the idea of "how long ago." On the recording, practice asking and answering how long ago something has been happening or how long ago it happened. Listen to the following exchanges on the recording.

¿Hace cuánto tiempo que lo conoces?	*How long have you known him?*
Lo conozco desde hace dos años.	*I have known him for two years.*
¿Hace cuánto tiempo que Uds. estudian?	*How long have you been studying?*
Hace seis meses que estudiamos.	*We've been studying for six months.*
¿Hace cuánto tiempo que Uds. viajaron a Guatemala?	*How long ago did you travel to Guatemala?*
Hace dos años que viajamos.	*We traveled two years ago.*

 ◄ **9.16** ►

Comprensión y expresión

¿Te diste cuenta? This is the way you ask "Did you realize?" or "Did you notice?" in Spanish. Be careful not to use the verb **realizar** in this case because, although this verb exists in Spanish, it actually means "to accomplish." When you want to say "to realize" or "to notice," use the verb **darse cuenta**. Listen to the following examples on the recording.

¿Te diste cuenta de que el guía no es mexicano?	*Did you realize that the guide is not Mexican?*
Sí, me di cuenta de que es muy inteligente también.	*Yes, I noticed that he is also very intelligent.*
¡No nos dimos cuenta de que la señora no comprende español!	*We didn't realize that the lady doesn't understand Spanish.*
Pero él se dio cuenta.	*But he noticed it.*
¿Te das cuenta de la situación?	*Do you realize the situation?*
Sí, me doy cuenta, pero ya es muy tarde.	*Yes, I realize it, but it is already very late.*

 ◄ **9.17** ►

DIALOG 3
De vuelta · *Going back*

Our friends are going back home. At this moment they are at the Mexican airport, going through the International Police booth where they get their passports stamped. Their trip to Mexico has come to an end, but it has been very rewarding. They have not only practiced their Spanish, learning a great deal in the process, but they have also seen interesting places and gathered valuable information about a Spanish-speaking country.

Anita y David están en el aeropuerto para tomar el vuelo de vuelta a los Estados Unidos. En este momento ellos pasan por Policía Internacional.

AGENTE	¿Cuántos días estuvieron en México?
ANITA	Estuvimos veinte días.
AGENTE	¿Qué ciudades visitaron?
DAVID	Visitamos la Ciudad de México, Oaxaca y Mérida.
ANITA	También estuvimos un par de días en Acapulco.
AGENTE	Muy bien. Aquí tienen sus pasaportes. ¡Buen viaje!
ANITA Y DAVID	¡Gracias! ¡Adiós!

 ◄ **9.18** ►
Expresión libre

Using what you have learned, answer the speaker in a spontaneous conversation that requires the use of the preterite tense.

◄ **9.19** ►
¡Viva la diferencia!

• The city of Oaxaca is located in the center of the state of Oaxaca, in the southernmost section of Mexico, next to the state of Chiapas. The Zapotecs and Mixtecs lived in the area thousands of years ago. Monte Albán was their capital.

The center of Oaxaca is the zócalo, with the cathedral on one of its corners. Five blocks away we find the Church of Santo Domingo, a fine example of Baroque style. Adjacent to the church is the former Convent of Santo Domingo, which today is the Museo Regional de Oaxaca. This museum features an awe-inspiring collection of gold and jade jewels found in the tombs of Monte Albán, as well as masks and costumes from the indigenous people who lived in the Oaxaca Valley.

• Chichén Itzá was a Mayan and Toltec center. In the center of these ruins there is a pyramid called El Castillo, the tallest building. At the top of this pyramid stands the temple of Kukulcan (the plumed serpent also known as Quetzalcoatl) that can be reached by climbing 91 steps. Actually, an even more ancient temple was discovered inside El Castillo. Another important part of these ruins is a ball court where ball games were played. These ball games had religious significance. One of the carvings at the ball court depicts a player being sacrificed.

◄ 9.20 ►
Pastimes

Congratulations! You have completed the course. As a treat, try these enjoyable puzzles.

Can you find the word that doesn't belong in each group?

1. amar, escribir, repetir, toalla, dormir

2. desayuno, cena, último, comida, almuerzo

3. carne, ventana, pollo, frutas, verduras

4. embarque, avión, piscina, mostrador, puerta de salida

5. propina, hambre, restaurante, cuenta, sueño

6. refresco, primavera, otoño, verano, invierno

7. catorce, cuatro, cuarenta, cámara, cincuenta

Riddles: Can you tell what it is?

1. ¿Qué cosa siempre va a llegar, pero nunca llega?

2. ¿Qué cosa se pierde, pero no se puede encontrar otra vez?

3. ¿Qué cosa tiene el mes de diciembre que no tiene ningún otro mes?

4. Nunca le pregunto nada a nadie, pero siempre me tienen que contestar.

5. Puedo correr y silbar (*whistle*), pero no tengo pies (*feet*) ni boca (*mouth*).

6. Estoy una vez en cada minuto, dos veces en cada momento, pero ninguna vez en cien años.

7. Puedo correr, pero no puedo caminar.

Can you guess the English equivalent of these idioms and proverbs?

1. Más vale tarde que nunca.

2. de mal en peor; de Guatemala en guatepeor

3. De tal palo, tal astilla.

4. ¡Vete a freír espárragos!

5. a la moda; en boga

6. a todo correr; como alma que se lleva el diablo

7. A la mejor cocinera se le quema la carne.

8. caer gordo

9. costar un ojo de la cara

10. Zapatero a tus zapatos.

Wonderword

All the words listed below appear in the puzzle—horizontally, vertically, diagonally, or even backward. Circle the letters. The leftover letters spell the wonderword, which has six letters.

```
Z  S  O  N  U  U  T  A  R  E  A
A  L  L  A  M  A  R  T  E  S  E
P  E  H  A  C  E  R  V  E  R  L
A  C  A  R  O  S  B  I  E  N  L
T  H  E  S  M  C  A  S  A  F  A
O  U  N  O  E  L  L  A  V  E  S
A  G  U  A  T  M  A  R  Z  O  O
C  A  L  R  E  O  R  E  N  E  L
O  P  O  I  R  E  S  A  S  S  O
M  P  R  E  S  I  D  E  N  T  E
O  E  O  S  I  E  U  Q  T  A  O
```

Wonderword _ _ _ _ _ _

agua	al	así	bien	caros	casa
come	como	ella	en	enero	esas
esto	feo	hacer	lechuga	león	loro
llamar	llaves	martes	marzo	mete	nulo
oír	presidente	que	se	si	solo
son	tapa	tarea	uno	ver	zapato

Can you name it?

1. Lo ponemos cuando hace calor.

   el _ _ _ _   _ _ _ _ _ _ _ _ _ _ _ _

2. La ponemos cuando hace frío.

   la _ _ _ _ _ _ _ _ _ _ _

3. Las tenemos cuando no trabajamos.

   las _ _ _ _ _ _ _ _ _ _

4. Lo tomamos en la mañana.

   el _ _ _ _ _ _ _ _

5. El mesero la recibe después de servir la comida.

   la _ _ _ _ _ _ _ ,

6. El arte de negociar los precios.

   el _ _ _ _ _ _ _

7. El mueble (*piece of furniture*) donde dormimos.

   la _ _ _ _

8. La cosa que tenemos que poner en la cámara.

   el _ _ _ _ _   _ _   _ _ _ _ _ _ _ _ _

9. La cosa donde ponemos nuestra ropa para viajar.

   la _ _ _ _ _ _

10. La bebida favorita de Moctezuma.

    el _ _ _ _ _ _ _ _ _

Answer key

1 En camino · *On the way*

1.14

TEACHER	Buenos días, John.
JOHN	Buenos días, señora Morales.
TEACHER	¿Qué tal?
JOHN	Soy de Nueva York.
TEACHER	¿Qué tal, cómo estás, John?
JOHN	Ah, perdón, muy bueno, gracias.
TEACHER	¡Muy bien, John, muy bien!
JOHN	¡Oh! ¡Sí! ¡Muy bien! ¡Muchas gracias!
TEACHER	De nada, John.

1.15   1. es   2. somos   3. es   4. soy   5. son   6. eres   7. son   8. es

1.16   1. Tú   2. Ella   3. Nosotros   4. Yo   5. Ellas   6. Él

1.17   1. Sí, ellos son de Bogotá.   2. Sí, él es jugador de tenis.
3. Sí, yo soy americano(-a).   4. Sí, nosotros somos de China. OR
No, nosotros no somos de China.   5. Sí, nosotros somos arquitectos.
6. Sí, él es de España.

1.18   1. doctor   2. receptionist   3. veterinarian   4. plumber
5. professor, teacher   6. mechanic   7. dentist   8. electrician
9. secretary   10. architect

1.20   1. inglesa   2. franceses   3. puertorriqueño   4. español
5. italiano   6. argentina   7. chino   8. cubano

1.21

¡Buenos días! ¿Cómo está usted?
¡Muy bien, gracias! (or other feeling)
Me llamo Carlos González. ¿Y usted?
Me llamo (your name).
Soy chileno. ¿Y usted?
Soy americano(-a). (or other nationality)
Soy profesor. ¿Y usted?
Soy abogado(-a). (or other profession)
Soy de Santiago de Chile. ¿De dónde es usted?
Soy de San Diego, de los Estados Unidos. (or other city)
¡Adiós!
¡Adiós!

2 ¡Me gusta aprender! · *I like to learn!*

2.4 1. 323-5417 2. 241-2246 3. 614-7064

2.5 1. Código de área seis, dieciocho–cuatro, setenta y seis, cincuenta y uno, veintitrés 2. Código de área dos, doce–dos, setenta, cero tres, sesenta y seis 3. Código de área cuatro, trece–siete, setenta y dos, ochenta y nueve, cuarenta y cinco

2.10

Mi dirección es calle (Avenida) _____ Número _____, (Apt. _____), (ciudad) _____.

1. Avenida Los Flamingos Nº 21, Apt. 4B (cuatro "be"), Quito 2. Calle Sánchez Nº 14, Bogotá 3. Calle Muñoz Nº 183, Apt. 3D, Caracas 4. Avenida Lavalle Nº 126, Apt. 54, Buenos Aires 5. Calle Los Limonares Nº 374, Valparaíso

2.11 1. ¿Cuál es tu número de teléfono? 2. ¿Cuál es tu dirección? 3. ¿Qué día es hoy? 4. ¿Qué fecha es hoy?

2.12 1. Los, la 2. Las, la 3. El, los 4. Los, el 5. El, la, el 6. Los, los

2.13 1. jueves cinco de agosto 2. lunes diecinueve de julio 3. viernes quince de enero 4. martes veinticinco de octubre 5. miércoles once de marzo

2.14

TEACHER   ¿Te gusta el español?
STUDENT   Me encanta el español y me encanta el profesora.
TEACHER   ¿Te encanta **la** profesora?
STUDENT   ¡Sí, señora! ¡Me encanta **la** profesora!

2.15

¡Hola! ¿Qué tal?
¡Hola! ¡Bien, gracias!
¿Cómo te llamas?
Me llamo (your name).
Te presento a mi amiga Catalina.
Mucho gusto, Catalina.
¿Cuál es tu dirección?
Vivo en la calle (street name) Número (house number), San Francisco, California (or other city).
¿Cuál es tu número de teléfono?
Mi número de teléfono es código de área cuatro, quince (or other area code); número cinco noventa, sesenta y dos, cero cuatro (or other number).
¿Qué tal tu clase?
Muy bien, gracias. Me encanta la clase.
¡Adiós!
¡Adiós!

3 ¡Me encanta este capítulo! · *I love this chapter!*

3.9 1. hablamos 2. trabajan 3. Miras 4. toca 5. preparan
6. canto 7. ama 8. escuchan

3.10 1. El, los 2. La, los 3. La 4. las 5. la 6. los 7. el 8. los

3.11 1. Compras, el, la 2. El, las, hablan 3. tocan, el 4. prepara, los
5. El, es

3.15 1. quinta 2. décima 3. primer 4. tercera 5. segundos

3.20 1. beben 2. comemos 3. comprendo 4. lee 5. Bebes
6. aprenden

3.21 1. vende, la 2. comprenden, el 3. aprendemos, el 4. leen, la
5. como, el 6. comprende, la 7. bebes

3.22

TEACHER ¿Te gusta el béisbol?
STUDENT ¡**Amo** el béisbol! ¡Ay! ¡Perdón! ¡Quiero decir **me encanta** el
  béisbol!
TEACHER Eres un estudiante excelente. ¡Bravo!

3.23

¿Te gusta el fútbol?
Sí, me gusta el fútbol. OR No, no me gusta el fútbol.
¿Hablas otra lengua (francés, italiano, etc.)?
Sí, hablo francés. OR No, no hablo otra lengua. OR Hablo sólo inglés y
español.
Yo trabajo en una oficina, ¿y tú?
Yo trabajo en una oficina también. (or other work location)
Yo soy abogado, ¿y tú?
Yo soy periodista. (or other profession)
¿Te gusta practicar español?
Sí, me gusta practicar español. OR Sí, me encanta practicar español. OR
No, no me gusta practicar español.
¿Aprenden español tus amigos?
Sí, mis amigos aprenden español también. OR No, mis amigos no
aprenden español.
¡Gracias y adiós!
¡Adiós!

4 De viaje · *On a trip*

4.14 1. estas 2. este 3. aquellos 4. ese 5. aquella 6. esa
4.15 1. una 2. unas 3. un 4. un 5. un 6. unos

4.16

PROFESORA	¿Escribe Ud. una carta?
ESTUDIANTE	No, escribo una tarjeta postal. ¿Cuántos sellos de cinco centavos hay que poner?
PROFESORA	Hay que poner tres sellos de cinco centavos.
ESTUDIANTE	¡Oh! ¡Estos sellos son de diez centavos!
PROFESORA	**Esos** sellos son de diez centavos, pero **éstos** son de cinco centavos.
ESTUDIANTE	Gracias por **estos** sellos.

4.17   1. estas puertas   2. este sello   3. estos asientos   4. esa señora
5. esas cartas   6. ese aeropuerto   7. esos pasajes   8. aquella profesora
9. aquel equipaje   10. aquellas tarjetas   11. aquellos profesores

4.19

¡Hola! ¿Qué tal?
Bien, gracias.

¿Haces las maletas?
No, no quiero hacer las maletas. OR Sí, hago las maletas.

¿Escribes una carta?
Sí, escribo una carta. OR No, no escribo una carta.

¿Necesitas un sello?
Sí, necesito un sello. OR No, no necesito un sello.

¿Tus amigos viven en aquella ciudad?
Mis amigos viven en Vancouver. (or other city)

¿Recibes una tarjeta postal de México?
Sí, recibo una tarjeta postal de México. OR No, no recibo una tarjeta postal de México.

¿Abres esta maleta o esa maleta?
Abro esta maleta. OR Abro esa maleta.

¿Te gusta ese asiento junto a la ventanilla o este asiento junto al pasillo?
Me gusta ese asiento. OR Me gusta este asiento.

5   Llegando al hotel · *Arriving at the hotel*

5.5   1. quieres   2. Quiero   3. quieren   4. Queremos   5. quieren
6. Queremos   7. Quiero   8. quieres   9. Quiero

5.6   1. 9:30 A.M.   2. 10:45 A.M.   3. 1:25 P.M.   4. 10:05 P.M.
5. 12 midnight   6. 2:50 A.M.

5.7   1. Son las dos y quince (cuarto) de la tarde.   2. Son las siete y
cuarenta y cinco de la mañana. (Son las ocho menos cuarto de la mañana.)
3. Son las cinco y veinticinco de la tarde.   4. Son las diez de la noche.
5. Es la una y cinco de la mañana.   6. Son las doce del día. (Es el
mediodía.)

5.13   1. tengo   2. tengo   3. tiene   4. tenemos   5. tienen

5.15   1. tengo sed   2. tenemos hambre   3. tenemos calor   4. tienes frío
5. tienes, Tengo   6. tengo miedo   7. tienes

5.18   1. Son las nueve y veinte de la noche.   2. Son las doce de la noche.
(Es la medianoche.)   3. Son las dos y cincuenta de la tarde. (Son las tres
menos diez de la tarde.)   4. El desayuno es a las siete y treinta (media) de
la mañana.   5. La cena es a las ocho de la noche.   6. El almuerzo es a la
una de la tarde.

5.22

Buenas tardes.
Buenas tardes. ¿En qué puedo servirlo?
¿Tiene una habitación disponible para una persona?
Sí. ¿Tiene usted una reservación?
No, no tengo una reservación.
¿Para cuántas noches?
Para esta noche solamente.
Tengo una habitación doble con baño privado.
¿Cuánto es la habitación?
La habitación es setecientos pesos.

¿Aló?
Aló.
¿En qué puedo servirlo?
Quisiera hacer una reservación. OR ¿Tiene una habitación?
¿Para cuántas personas?
Para una. OR Para dos personas. (or other number)
¿Para qué fecha?
Para el próximo lunes, cinco de octubre, hasta el miércoles, ocho de
octubre. (or other dates)

6   En el hotel · *At the hotel*

6.6   1. Te, me   2. gustaría, me   3. Te gustaría, me   4. Te gustaría
5. gustaría, me

6.8   1. Sí, los veo.   2. Sí, lo veo.   3. Sí, las veo.   4. Sí, lo veo.
5. Sí, los veo.   6. Sí, lo veo.   7. Sí, la veo.   8. Sí, lo veo.

6.19   1. ¿Puedes arreglarlo?   2. ¿Quieres comerlas?   3. ¿La puedo
mandar ahora?   4. ¿Puedes llevarlas?   5. ¿Puedes llamarlos?

6.21   1. quieren   2. podemos   3. juegas   4. sirve   5. quiero
6. juegan   7. jugamos   8. puede

6.22

Hay una piscina allí. ¿Quieres verla?
Sí, la quiero ver. OR No, no quiero verla. (or variants)

La calefacción no funciona. ¿Puedes arreglarla?
No, no la puedo arreglar. OR Sí, puedo arreglarla. (or variants)
Me gustaría escribir una carta. ¿Puedes mandarla?
Sí, la puedo mandar. OR No, no puedo mandarla. (or variants)
Esa chica se llama Eugenia. ¿Carlos la quiere?
Sí, Carlos la quiere. OR No, Carlos no la quiere. (or variants)
Yo no quiero mover mi silla. ¿Quieres mover tu silla?
No, no la quiero mover. OR Sí, quiero moverla. (or variants)
En ese restaurante sirven unos platos deliciosos ¿Quieres comerlos?
Sí, los quiero comer. OR No, no quiero comerlos. (or variants)

7 En el restaurante · *At the restaurant*

7.6   1. se   2. nos   3. se   4. se   5. te   6. me   7. se

7.7   1. se sienta   2. me duermo   3. se sientan   4. nos sentamos
5. se duermen   6. se duerme   7. se lava   8. te secas   9. nos dormimos
10. nos sentamos

7.14   1. para ella   2. para nosotros   3. para Ud.   4. con ellos
5. contigo   6. con ellos   7. conmigo

7.19   1. estoy   2. están   3. está   4. estamos   5. están   6. estás
7. está   8. está   9. están   10. está

7.20

¿Qué te trae el mesero para beber?
El mesero me trae vino blanco. (or other drink)

¿Qué le pides al mesero de postre?
Le pido los pasteles a él. (or other dessert)

¿Para quién es la ensalada de lechuga?
Ella es para mi madre. (or other dining companion)

¿Qué le pides al mesero después de comer?
Le pido la cuenta.

¿Adónde van a ir Uds. después de comer en el restaurante?
Vamos a ir al teatro después de comer allí. (or other place)

¿Vas a menudo a un restaurante mexicano?
Sí, voy a menudo a un restaurante mexicano. OR No, no voy a menudo.

¿Estás ocupado (busy) ahora?
Sí, estoy ocupado(-a). OR No, no estoy ocupado(-a).

7.21

ESTUDIANTE	Señora, si quiero decir "I am at home", ¿digo *soy en casa* o *estoy en casa*?
PROFESORA	Dices *estoy en casa.* Cuando quieres decir *dónde,* usas *estar.*
ESTUDIANTE	¡Ah! Entonces, ¿es correcto *estoy triste* o *soy triste*?
PROFESORA	*Estoy triste* es correcto. ¡Es una condición!

8 Por la ciudad · *Around the city*

8.5 1. Quiero tomar dos aspirinas porque me duele la cabeza.
2. Si camino mucho, me van a doler los pies.   3. No me molesta limpiar
la casa. (Sí, me molesta...)   4. No les importa ir en autobús. (Sí, les
importa...)   5. Si como mucho, me duele el estómago.   6. No me
importa comer tarde. (Sí, me importa...)   7. No nos molesta caminar a
casa. (Sí, nos molesta...)

8.8 1. tengo que   2. tiene que   3. tienen que   4. tenemos que
5. tienes que   6. Hay que   7. Hay que

8.15 1. van   2. hago   3. vienes   4. valen   5. damos   6. tienen
7. salgo   8. hacen   9. doy

8.17 1. está   2. están   3. es   4. es, Es   5. estamos   6. están   7. está
8. es   9. son

8.22 1. sé   2. oyen   3. decimos   4. traes   5. pone   6. traigo
7. caigo   8. sabe   9. conozco

8.24 1. un coche bueno   2. un mal perdedor   3. unos zapatos caros
4. el mejor precio   5. una blusa blanca   6. un vendedor viejo

8.25

¿Te importa contestar estas preguntas?
Sí, me importa contestarlas. OR No, no me importa contestarlas.

¿Es más grande o más pequeña la ciudad de México que Madrid?
La ciudad de México es más grande que Madrid. OR Es más grande
que Madrid.

¿Qué eres?
Soy doctor. (or other description)

¿Cómo eres?
Soy alto(-a) e inteligente. (or other characteristics)

¿Sabes hablar otra lengua?
Sí, sé hablar francés. (or other languages)

¿Conoces la ciudad de México?
No, no la conozco. OR Sí, la conozco.

¿Te gusta regatear?
Sí, me gusta regatear. OR No, no me gusta regatear.

¿Qué necesitas hacer si quieres ir en una gira turística?
Necesito hacer una reservación. OR Tengo que hacer una reservación.

9 Lo pasamos muy bien · *We had a great time*

9.5 1. ayudó   2. compró   3. hablé   4. estudiamos   5. limpiaste
6. cantaron   7. gustó   8. invitaron   9. pasaron

9.7 1. escribió   2. comieron   3. hablé   4. vivimos   5. explicó
6. abriste   7. compré   8. Leíste   9. comprendieron   10. abrió

9.14 1. dieron 2. tuvo 3. dijo 4. tuvimos 5. hizo 6. di 7. diste
8. Fue 9. fueron 10. estuvieron 11. fue

9.18

¿Lo pasaron bien Anita y David en México?
Sí, lo pasaron bien allí.

A propósito de pasarlo bien, ¿se dio cuenta Ud. de que terminamos el libro?
No, no me di cuenta que lo terminamos. OR Sí, me di cuenta que
lo terminamos.

¿Qué le gustó más? ¿Por qué?
Me gustó aprender la lengua y la cultura porque son interesantes.
(Answers will vary.)

¿Hace cuánto tiempo que empezó (start) *a estudiar español?*
Hace dos años que empecé a estudiarlo. (or other time ago)

¿Estuvo alguna vez en México?
Sí, estuve alguna vez allí. OR No, no estuve nunca allí.

¿Tuvo problema con su pasaporte alguna vez?
No, no tuve nunca problema con mi pasaporte.

¿Comprendió Ud. qué quiso decir el agente cuando dijo "buen viaje"?
Sí, comprendí lo que quiso decir. OR No, no comprendí lo que quiso decir.

9.20

Can you find the word that doesn't belong?

1. toalla (not a verb) 2. último (not a meal) 3. ventana (not food)
4. piscina (not found at the airport) 5. sueño (not found at a restaurant)
6. refresco (not a season) 7. cámara (not a number)

Riddles

1. mañana 2. el tiempo 3. la letra "d" 4. el teléfono 5. el viento
6. la letra "m" 7. el agua

Can you guess the English equivalent of these idioms and proverbs?

1. Better late than never. 2. from bad to worse 3. Like father, like son.
(From such wood, such splinter.) 4. Get lost! (Go fry asparagus!)
5. in style, the "in" thing 6. at breakneck speed 7. Everybody makes
mistakes. 8. to be a pain in the neck 9. to cost a mint 10. Mind your
own business.

Wonderword

puerta

Can you name it?

1. el aire acondicionado 2. la calefacción 3. las vacaciones
4. el desayuno 5. la propina 6. el regateo 7. la cama 8. el rollo de
película 9. la maleta 10. el chocolate

Grammar summary

El alfabeto

Pronunciation of the letter name is in parentheses.

a   (ah) Ana, mamá, papá
b   (be) bebé
c   (se) c + a, o, u = /k/ casa, cosa, culto
        c + e, i = /s/ cesta, cine
d   (de) dentista, todo
e   (eh) bebé, lee, elegante
f   (efe) elefante
g   (heh) g + a, o, u = /g/ gato, gota, gusto
        g + e, i = harsh /j/ gente, gitano
        gu + e, i = soft /g/ guerra, guitarra
h   (ah-che) silent: hotel, almohada
        c + h = /ch/ chico
i   (ee) Mimí, sí
j   (hota) jabón, Juan
k   (ka) kiosco
l   (ele) laguna
ll (eh-ye [like the *y* in the English word "yet"]) llave, calle
m   (eme) María
n   (ene) no
ñ   (enye) España
o   (oh) Oscar, no, tonto
p   (pe) papá
q   (koo) (only in the combination *que* or *qui*) qu = /k/ queso, máquina
r   (ere) pero
rr (erre) (rolled) perro
s   (ese) solo
t   (te) Teresa
u   (ue [as in "Sue"]) Ursula, cucú
v   (veh) There is no difference in pronunciation between **b** and **v**:
        Verónica
w   (doh-ble veh) Walter
x   (e-kees) examen
y   (ee gree-eh-ga) tuyo
z   (seh-tah) Zaragoza

Be sure to pronounce each part of each word. Each syllable has the same length, but there is an emphasis on one syllable in a word. The emphasis is on the second-to-last syllable if the word ends in a vowel or **n** or **s**. The emphasis is on the last syllable if the word ends in a consonant other than **n** or **s**. Words that are exceptions to these rules have a written accent (*máquina, ¿Dónde?, solución*).

La puntuación

In Spanish you must use a question mark at the beginning of the question as well as at the end, and an exclamation point at both the beginning and the end of an exclamatory sentence (*¿De dónde eres? ¡Muy bien!*).

Los números

Cardinales

1	uno	11	once	21	veintiuno (veinte y uno)
2	dos	12	doce	29	veintinueve
3	tres	13	trece	30	treinta
4	cuatro	14	catorce	40	cuarenta
5	cinco	15	quince	50	cincuenta
6	seis	16	dieciséis	60	sesenta
7	siete	17	diecisiete	70	setenta
8	ocho	18	dieciocho	80	ochenta
9	nueve	19	diecinueve	90	noventa
10	diez	20	veinte	100	cien

101	ciento uno	10.000	diez mil
200	doscientos	100.000	cien mil
300	trescientos	1.000.000	un millón
400	cuatrocientos		
500	quinientos		
600	seiscientos		
700	setecientos		
800	ochocientos		
900	novecientos		
1000	mil		

Note: Numbers between 16 and 29 can be written two different ways.

dieciséis	diez y seis
veintidós	veinte y dos
veinticuatro	veinte y cuatro
veintiocho	veinte y ocho

Also note: cien (100), BUT cie**nto** uno, cie**nto** noventa, etc.
mil (1000), BUT **un** millón (1000000)

Ordinales

1°	primero	6°	sexto
2°	segundo	7°	séptimo
3°	tercero	8°	octavo
4°	cuarto	9°	noveno
5°	quinto	10°	décimo

Ordinal numbers can be masculine or feminine, singular or plural, according to the noun they modify.

el primer capítulo (drop the -o in *primero* and *tercero*)   la primera señora
los primeros capítulos   las primeras señoras

Pronouns

Subject of a verb

yo	*I*
tú	*you (familiar)*
él	*he*
ella	*she*
usted (Ud.)	*you (formal)*
nosotros	*we*
vosotros*	*you (plural)*
ellos	*they (masculine)*
ellas	*they (feminine)*
ustedes (Uds.)	*you (plural)*

After a preposition

(para, por, a, en, de)

(para)	mí**	*(for) me*
	ti**	*you*
	él	*him*
	ella	*her*
	usted	*you*
	nosotros	*us*
	vosotros	*you*
	ellos	*them*
	ellas	*them*
	ustedes	*you*

***Vosotros** is used in Spain.
BUT **conmigo ("with me"), **contigo** ("with you").

Objects of a verb

DIRECT		INDIRECT	
me	*me*	me	*to me*
te	*you (familiar)*	te	*to you (familiar)*
lo	*him, you (formal), it*	le	*to him, to you (formal)*
la	*her, you (formal), it*	le	*to her, to you (formal)*
nos	*us*	nos	*to us*
os	*you (Spain)*	os	*to you (plural)*
los	*them, you (formal, plural)*	les	*to them, to you (formal, plural)*

Reflexive pronouns

me	*myself*
te	*yourself (familiar)*
se	*himself, herself, yourself (formal)*
nos	*ourselves*
os	*yourselves (Spain)*
se	*themselves, yourselves (formal, plural)*

Verbs

Present tense

REGULAR VERBS

Remember: Verbs end in **-ar**, **-er**, or **-ir**. A regular verb changes only the ending.

-ar	**hablar**	
-o	yo hablo	*I speak*
-as	tú hablas	*you speak*
-a	él, ella, usted habla	*he, she speaks, you speak*
-amos	nosotros hablamos	*we speak*
-áis	vosotros habláis	*you speak*
-an	ellos, ellas, ustedes hablan	*they, you speak*

-er	**aprender**
-o	yo aprendo
-es	tú aprendes
-e	él, ella, usted aprende
-emos	nosotros aprendemos
-éis	vosotros aprendéis
-en	ellos, ellas, ustedes aprenden

-ir	**vivir**
-o	yo vivo
-es	tú vives
-e	él, ella, usted vive
-imos	nosotros vivimos
-ís	vosotros vivís
-en	ellos, ellas, ustedes viven

IRREGULAR VERBS

SER ("to be")	ESTAR ("to be in a place or condition")
soy	estoy
eres	estás
es	está
somos	estamos
sois	estáis
son	están

IR ("to go")	DAR ("to give")	HACER ("to do, make")
voy	doy	hago
vas	das	haces
va	da	hace
vamos	damos	hacemos
vais	dais	hacéis
van	dan	hacen

SALIR ("to go out")	VENIR ("to come")	TENER ("to have")
salgo	vengo	tengo
sales	vienes	tienes
sale	viene	tiene
salimos	venimos	tenemos
salís	venís	tenéis
salen	vienen	tienen

DECIR ("to say")	OÍR ("to hear")	CONOCER ("to know")
digo	oigo	conozco
dices	oyes	conoces
dice	oye	conoce
decimos	oímos	conocemos
decís	oís	conocéis
dicen	oyen	conocen

STEM-CHANGING VERBS

o>ue

MOVER ("to move")	MORIR ("to die")	DORMIR ("to sleep")
muevo	muero	duermo
mueves	mueres	duermes
mueve	muere	duerme
movemos	morimos	dormimos
movéis	morís	dormís
mueven	mueren	duermen

PODER ("to be able")

puedo
puedes
puede
podemos
podéis
pueden

e>ie

QUERER ("to want")	PENSAR ("to think")	SENTAR ("to sit")
quiero	pienso	siento
quieres	piensas	sientas
quiere	piensa	sienta
queremos	pensamos	sentamos
queréis	pensáis	sentáis
quieren	piensan	sientan

SENTIR ("to feel")

siento
sientes
siente
sentimos
sentís
sienten

e>i

PEDIR ("to ask for")	SERVIR ("to serve")	REPETIR ("to repeat")
pido	sirvo	repito
pides	sirves	repites
pide	sirve	repite
pedimos	servimos	repetimos
pedís	servís	repetís
piden	sirven	repiten

u>ue

JUGAR ("to play [a game]")

juego
juegas
juega
jugamos
jugáis
juegan

REFLEXIVE VERBS

LAVARSE ("to wash oneself")

me lavo
te lavas
se lava
nos lavamos
os laváis
se lavan

SECARSE ("to dry oneself")

me seco
te secas
se seca
nos secamos
os secáis
se secan

DORMIRSE ("to fall asleep")

me duermo
te duermes
se duerme
nos dormimos
os dormís
se duermen

SENTARSE ("to sit down")

me siento
te sientas
se sienta
nos sentamos
os sentáis
se sientan

SENTIRSE ("to feel")

me siento
te sientes
se siente
nos sentimos
os sentís
se sienten

Past tense (Preterite)

REGULAR VERBS

-ar	hablar	-er, -ir	comer	escribir
-é	hablé	-í	comí	escribí
-aste	hablaste	-iste	comiste	escribiste
-ó	habló	-ió	comió	escribió
-amos	hablamos	-imos	comimos	escribimos
-asteis	hablasteis	-isteis	comisteis	escribisteis
-aron	hablaron	-ieron	comieron	escribieron

IRREGULAR VERBS

SER/IR	ESTAR
fui	estuve
fuiste	estuviste
fue	estuvo
fuimos	estuvimos
fuisteis	estuvisteis
fueron	estuvieron

TENER	DAR	HACER
tuve	di	hice
tuviste	diste	hiciste
tuvo	dio	hizo
tuvimos	dimos	hicimos
tuvisteis	disteis	hicisteis
tuvieron	dieron	hicieron

VER	OÍR	LEER
vi	oí	leí
viste	oíste	leíste
vio	oyó	leyó
vimos	oímos	leímos
visteis	oísteis	leísteis
vieron	oyeron	leyeron

STEM-CHANGING VERBS

DORMIR	SERVIR	REPETIR
dormí	serví	repetí
dormiste	serviste	repetiste
durmió	sirvió	repitió
dormimos	servimos	repetimos
dormisteis	servisteis	repetisteis
durmieron	sirvieron	repitieron

VERBS WITH SPELLING CHANGES IN THE *YO* FORM

EXPLICAR	PRACTICAR	SACAR
expliqué	practiqué	saqué
explicaste	practicaste	sacaste
explicó	practicó	sacó
explicamos	practicamos	sacamos
explicasteis	practicasteis	sacasteis
explicaron	practicaron	sacaron

TOCAR	JUGAR	PAGAR
toqué	jugué	pagué
tocaste	jugaste	pagaste
tocó	jugó	pagó
tocamos	jugamos	pagamos
tocasteis	jugasteis	pagasteis
tocaron	jugaron	pagaron

Spanish-English glossary

This glossary includes the vocabulary presented in the text.

Abbreviations used in this glossary

fam.	familiar	*obj. pron.*	object pronoun
fem.	feminine	*pl.*	plural
inf.	infinitive	*prep.*	preposition
irreg.	irregular verb	*pron.*	pronoun
masc.	masculine	*sing.*	singular

How to find the form you need

Nouns Unmarked nouns ending in -o are masculine; unmarked nouns ending in -a are feminine. Other nouns and exceptions to this rule are marked for gender with the appropriate definite article, **(el)** for masculine nouns and **(la)** for feminine nouns, for example, **tren (el)** and **habitación (la)**.

Plurals The plural form of nouns and adjectives is not included in the glossary. Use this guide to form the plural.
* Nouns and adjectives ending in -o, -a, and -e form the plural by adding -s.
* Nouns and adjectives ending in a consonant other than -z form the plural by adding -es.
* Nouns and adjectives ending in -z form the plural by changing the z to c and adding -es.
* The stress remains the same in the plural as in the singular. Accent marks will, therefore, need to be added or deleted as necessary.

Verbs Unmarked infinitives are regular. The abbreviation (*irreg.*) follows the infinitives of irregular verbs. Infinitives of stem-changing verbs are followed by (o>ue), (e>ie), or (e>i) as appropriate. Examples of these notations are **decir** (*irreg.*), **almorzar** (o>ue), **comenzar** (e>ie), and **repetir** (e>i).

a to
a causa de due to
a la plancha grilled
a la una en punto at one on the dot
a las dos at two o'clock
a menudo often
(a mí) me gusta I like
a propósito by the way
a propósito de speaking of

¿a qué hora es ____? at what time is ____?
(a ti) te gusta you like
a veces sometimes
abogado(-a) lawyer
abril (el) April
abrir to open
aburrido(-a) boring, bored
acabar to finish
accidente (el) accident

aceituna olive
aceptar to accept
además besides
adiós good-bye
adónde where to
aerolínea airline
aeropuerto airport
agencia agency
agente (el/la) agent
agosto August
agregar to add
agua (el) (*fem.*) water
ahora now
ahora mismo right away
aire (el) acondicionado
  air-conditioning
alfombra rug, carpet
algo something
algo más something else
allí there
almeja clam
almorzar (o>ue) to have lunch
almuerzo lunch
alrededores (los) outskirts
alto(-a) tall
alumno(-a) student, pupil
amable kind
amar to love
americano(-a) American
amigo(-a) male friend, female friend
anoche last night
anotar to write down
antes before
antiguo(-a) ancient
anuncio advertisement
apartamento apartment
aprender to learn
aquí here
argentino(-a) Argentine
arquitecto(-a) architect
arreglar to fix
arroz (el) rice
arte (el) art
artista (el/la) artist
artístico(-a) artistic
ascensor (el) elevator
asiento seat
auto car
autobús bus

auxiliar de vuelo (el/la) flight
  attendant
avenida avenue
avión (el) airplane
ayer yesterday

bailarín (el), bailarina (la) dancer
bajar to go down
bajar de to get off
balcón (el) balcony
baloncesto basketball
banana banana
baño bathroom
barato(-a) inexpensive
barroco(-a) Baroque
bastante enough
beber to drink
bebida drink
béisbol (el) baseball
biblioteca library
bicicleta bicycle
bien well
bienvenidos a ___ welcome to ___
billete (el) ticket
bistec (el) steak
blanco(-a) white
blusa blouse
bonito(-a) beautiful
bordado(-a) embroidered
botella bottle
botones (el) bellboy
buenas noches good night
buenas tardes good afternoon;
  good evening
bueno(-a) good
buenos días good morning

cabeza head
cada each
caer (*irreg.*) to fall
calculadora calculator
calle (la) street
calor (el) heat
cama bed
cámara camera
camarera chambermaid, waitress
camarero waiter
camarones (los) shrimp (used in
  Latin America)

caminar to walk
campo countryside, field
candidato(-a) candidate
cangrejo crab
cansado(-a) tired
cantante (el, la) singer
cantar to sing
caro(-a) expensive
carta letter
casa house
casado(-a) married
castillo castle
cena dinner, supper
cenar to have dinner
centro center
cerca near, close
cereza cherry
cerveza beer
chao good-bye (*informal*)
chile (el) pepper
chileno(-a) Chilean
chocolate (el) chocolate
cine (el) cinema, movies
cinturón (el) de seguridad seat belt
ciudad (la) city
clase (la) class
clásico(-a) classic
clavadista (el/la) diver
coche (el) car
cocinero(-a) cook, chef
código de área area code
colombiano(-a) Colombian
comedor (el) dining room
comenzar (o>ue) to begin
comida food
¿cómo? how?
¿cómo estás? how are you?
cómodo(-a) comfortable
completo(-a) complete, full
comprar to buy
comprender to understand
computadora computer
con with
concierto concert
condición (la) condition
conmigo with me
conocer to know places or people
contigo with you
corbata necktie

correcto(-a) correct
correr to run
cosa thing
crédito credit
creer to believe
cuaderno notebook
¿cuál? which?, what?
cuando when
¿cuándo? when?
¿cuánto? how much?
¿cuántos(-as)? how many?
cuarto(-a) fourth
cubano(-a) Cuban
cucaracha cockroach
cuchara spoon
cucharita teaspoon
cuchillo knife
cuenta bill, account
¡cuidado! careful!

dar (*irreg.*) to give
dar un paseo to take a walk or ride
darse cuenta to realize
datar to date from
de of, from
de nada you are welcome
deber must, to have to
decidir to decide
décimo(-a) tenth
decir (*irreg.*) to say
decorar to adorn
dejar to leave something behind
delicioso(-a) delicious
dentista (el/la) dentist
desayuno breakfast
descansar to rest
desde from, since
desear to wish
desocupar to vacate
después after, afterward
detallado(-a) detailed
día (el) day
diciembre (el) December
dinero money
dirección (la) address
disfrutar to enjoy
disponible available
doble double
doctor (el), doctora (la) doctor

dólar (el) dollar
doler (o>ue) to ache, hurt
domingo Sunday
¿dónde? where?
dormido(-a) asleep
dormir (o>ue) to sleep
dormirse (o>ue) to fall asleep
dueño(-a) owner
durante during
durazno peach

el the
él he
electricista (el/la) electrician
ella she
ellas they (*fem.*)
ellos they (*masc.*)
embarcar to board
embarque (el) boarding
en in, on, at
en efectivo cash
en seguida right away
encantado(-a) delighted
encantar to enchant
enchilada rolled tortilla filled with cheese, chicken or meat
encontrar (o>ue) to find
encontrarse (o>ue) to meet
enero January
enojarse to get mad
ensalada salad
entrada entrance, theatre ticket
entrar to enter
entrevista interview
entusiasmado(-a) excited, enthusiastic
equipaje (el) luggage
equipaje (el) de mano hand luggage
escoger to choose
escribir to write
escritorio desk
escuchar to listen
escuela school
eso that
España Spain
español (el) Spanish (language)
español, española Spanish
especial special

esposo(-a) husband, wife
estar (*irreg.***)** to be (in a place or condition)
esto this
estómago stomach
estudiante (el/la) student
estupendo(-a) marvelous
exagerar to overdo

fábrica factory
fantástico(-a) fantastic
favor de + *inf.* please, do ____
favorito(-a) favorite
febrero February
fecha date
fideos (los) noodles
fiesta party, celebration
figurita figurine
filarmónica philharmonic
filete (el) de merluza fillet of hake
finalmente finally
flan (el) custard
francés (el) French (language)
francés, francesa French
fresa strawberry
fresco(-a) cool, fresh
frijol (el) bean
frío cold
frito(-a) fried
fruta fruit
fumar to smoke
función (la) performance
funcionar to work (machines)
fútbol (el) soccer

gambas shrimp (used in Spain)
generalmente generally
gimnasio gym
gira tour
gótico(-a) Gothic
gracias thank you
grande big
grupo group
guacamole (el) mashed avocado with tomato and onion
guía (el/la) guide

habitación (la) room
hablar to speak

hacer (*irreg.*) to do, to make
hacer ejercicio to exercise
hacer las maletas to pack
hacer planes to make plans
hambre (el) (*fem.*) hunger
hasta until
hasta la vista till I see you
hay (*irreg.*) there is, there are
hay que one must
helado ice cream
hermoso(-a) beautiful
histórico(-a) historic, historical
hora hour, time
horriblemente horribly
hospedaje (el) lodging
hospedarse to take lodging
hotel (el) hotel
hoy today
huachinango red snapper

idea idea
iglesia church
importar to matter
imposible impossible
impresionante impressive
impuesto tax
incluido(-a) included
incluir to include
infinitivo infinitive
información (la) information
informe (el) report
ingeniero(-a) engineer
inglés (el) English (language)
inglés, inglesa English
ingrediente (el) ingredient
inmediatamente right away
inteligente intelligent
interesante interesting
internacional international
invierno winter
ir (*irreg.*) to go
italiano(-a) Italian

jade (el) jade
joya jewel
jueves (el) Thursday
jugador (el), jugadora (la) player
jugar (u>ue) to play (a game)
jugo juice

julio July
junio June

lanzarse to dive
lápiz pencil
lavar to wash
lechuga lettuce
leer to read
lengua language, tongue
libreta small notebook
libro book
limonada lemonade
literatura literature
llamar to call
llave (la) key
llegar to arrive
llevar to carry, to take along
lo siento I am sorry
locutor (el), locutora (la) announcer
los/las the (*pl.*)
luego later, afterwards
lunes (el) Monday

macho virile
mal bad, badly, ill
maleta suitcase
maletín (el) briefcase
malo(-a) bad
mañana tomorrow
mañana (la) morning
mar (el) sea
marfil (el) ivory
martes (el) Tuesday
marzo March
más plus, more
más o menos so-so
maya (el/la) Mayan
mayo May
mayor older
me me, to me, myself
me encanta I love (a thing or an activity)
me gusta I like
me gustaría I would like
mecánico(-a) mechanic
medianoche (la) midnight
medio(-a) half
mediodía (el) noon
mejor better, best

menor younger
menos less
mentir (e>ie) to lie
menú (el) menu
mercado market
mes (el) month
mesa table
mesero(-a) waiter, waitress
metro subway
mexicano(-a) Mexican
mezclar to mix
mi my
mientras while
miércoles (el) Wednesday
minuto minute
mío(-a) mine
mirar to look at, to watch
mitad (la) half
mocho(-a) cut off, cropped
molestar to bother
momento moment
monumento monument
morir (o>ue) to die
mostrador (el) counter
mover (o>ue) to move
mozo waiter
muchas gracias thank you very much
mucho(-a) a lot of, much
mucho gusto pleased to meet you
muchos(-as) many
museo museum
música music
muy very

nada nothing
nada más nothing else
nadar to swim
naranja orange
necesitar to need
niño(-a) child
noche (la) night
nos us, to us, ourselves
nosotros we
noticias news
novela novel
noveno(-a) ninth
noviembre (el) November
nuestro(-a) our
nuevo(-a) new

nuez (la) walnut
número number
nunca never

octavo(-a) eighth
octubre (el) October
ocupado(-a) busy, occupied
oficina office
ofrecer to offer
oír (*irreg.***)** to hear
olvidar to forget
oro gold
otoño fall (season)
otro(-a) other, another

padre (el) father
padres (los) parents
pagar to pay
país (el) country, nation
palacio palace
papel (el) paper
par (el) pair, couple
para in order to, for
pared (la) wall
parque (el) park
partida departure
pasado(-a) past
pasaje (el) ticket
pasaje de ida y vuelta round-trip
   ticket
pasaporte (el) passport
pasar por to pass through
pasarlo bien to have a good time
paseo walk, ride
pasillo aisle, corridor
patio yard, courtyard
patrón (el), patrona (la) patron
   saint
pedido order
pedir (e>i) to ask for
peluquero(-a) hairdresser
pensar (e>ie) to think
peor worse
perdedor (el), perdedora (la) loser
perder (e>ie) to lose
perderse (e>ie) to get lost
perdón excuse me
periódico newspaper
periodista (el/la) journalist

perla pearl
permitir to allow
peruano(-a) Peruvian
peso monetary unit of some Latin
  American countries
piano piano
picadillo de pollo chicken hash
picante spicy, hot
pie (el) foot
piña pineapple
pirámide (la) pyramid
piscina swimming pool
piso floor
plata silver
plato dish
playa beach
plomero(-a) plumber
pobre poor
poco little, small amount
poder (o>ue) to be able
policía police
pollo chicken
poner (*irreg.*) to put
ponerse (*irreg.*) to become, to get
popular popular
poquito little bit
por for, by, through
por favor please
¿por qué? why?
por suerte luckily
por supuesto of course
porción (la) portion
porque because
postre (el) dessert
practicar to practice
precio price
preferir (e>ie) to prefer
pregunta question
preguntar to ask
preparado(-a) prepared
preparar to prepare
presentar to introduce someone
presidente (el), presidenta (la)
  president
primavera spring
primero(-a) first
princesa princess
privado(-a) private
probar (o>ue) to taste

problema (el) problem
profesor (el), profesora (la)
  professor, teacher
programa (el) program
pronto soon
propina tip
próximo(-a) next
puerta door
puerta de salida departure gate
pulsera bracelet
punto dot, point, period

que that
¿qué? what?
¿qué tal? how are things?
querer (e>ie) to want, to love
querer (e>ie) decir to mean
queso cheese
quinto(-a) fifth
quisiera I would like

rápido(-a) fast
recepción (la) reception desk
recepcionista (el/la) receptionist
recibir to receive
recomendar (e>ie) to recommend
recordar (o>ue) to remember
refresco cold drink
regatear to bargain
regatón (el), regatona (la) haggler
regresar to come back
relleno(-a) stuffed
repetir (e>i) to repeat
reservación (la) reservation
restaurante (el) restaurant
revisar to check
revista magazine
rojo(-a) red
rollo de película roll of film
ruinas ruins
ruso(-a) Russian

sábado Saturday
saber (*irreg.*) to know
sagrado(-a) holy, sacred
sal (la) salt
salida departure, exit
salir (*irreg.*) to go out
salsa sauce

sarape (el) serape
se himself, herself, yourself (Ud.),
   yourselves (Uds.), themselves
se + *obj. pron.* to him, to her, to you,
   to them
secador (el) de pelo hair dryer
secar to dry
secretario(-a) secretary
sed (la) thirst
segundo(-a) second
sello stamp
señor (el) Mr., gentleman, sir
señora Mrs., woman, lady
señorita Miss, young woman,
   young lady
sentado(-a) sitting, seated
sentar (e>ie) to sit
sentir (e>ie) to feel
separarse to separate
septiembre (el) September
séptimo(-a) seventh
ser (*irreg.*) to be
servicio service
servir (e>i) to serve
sexto(-a) sixth
si if, whether
sí yes
siempre always
silla chair
simpático(-a) nice
sin without
situación (la) situation
sol (el) sun
solamente only
solo alone
sólo only
soltero(-a) single, unmarried
sombrero hat
sopa soup
su his, her, your, their
subir to climb, to go up
sueño sleep
surtido(-a) mixed

tamal (el) tamale, Mexican dish
también also
tanto(-a) so much, as much
tarde late
tarde (la) afternoon

tarea homework, task
tarjeta de crédito credit card
tarjeta postal postcard
taxi (el) taxi
te you, to you
te presento a _____ I'd like you to
   meet _____
teatro theater
techo roof, ceiling
tele (la) TV
teléfono telephone
televisión (la) television
templo temple
tenedor (el) fork
tener (*irreg.*) to have
tener _____ años to be _____ years
   old
tener calor to be hot, warm
tener frío to be cold
tener ganas to feel like
tener hambre to be hungry
tener miedo to be afraid
tener prisa to be in a hurry
tener razón to be right
tener sueño to be sleepy
tenis (el) tennis
tercero(-a) third
terminal (el) terminal
terminar to finish
terrible terrible
tesoro treasure
tiempo weather, time
típico(-a) typical, traditional
toalla towel
tocar to play (an instrument)
tolteca (el/la) Toltec
tomar to take
tomar fotos to take pictures
tomate (el) tomato
tortilla round, unleavened bread
   (Latin America), omelet (Spain)
total (el) total
trabajar to work
traer (*irreg.*) to bring
tren (el) train
triste sad
tu your
tú you (*sing.*, *fam.*)
turístico(-a) touristic, tourist

último(-a) last
universidad (la) university, college
uno(-a) one, a
usted you (*sing., formal*)
ustedes you (*pl.*)

vacaciones (las) vacation,
  vacations
valer (*irreg.*) to be worth
vaso drinking glass
vendedor, vendedora vendor
vender to sell
venezolano(-a) Venezuelan
venir (*irreg.*) to come
ventana window
ventanilla small window
ver (*irreg.*) to see
verano summer
verdad (la) truth
¿verdad? isn't that so?
verduras fresh vegetables
vermut (el) vermouth
veterinario(-a) veterinarian

vez (la) time (as in one time, once)
viajar to travel
viaje (el) travel, trip
viaje de ida y vuelta round-trip
viejo(-a) old
viento wind
viernes (el) Friday
vino blanco white wine
violín (el) violin
visitar to visit
vista view
vivir to live
volver (o>ue) to come back, to
  return
vosotros you (*pl.*) (used in Spain)
vuelta return

ya already
yo I

zapato shoe
zapoteca (el/la) Zapotec Indian
zócalo public square

English-Spanish glossary

This glossary includes the vocabulary presented in the text.

Abbreviations used in this glossary

fam.	familiar	*obj. pron.*	object pronoun
fem.	feminine	*pl.*	plural
inf.	infinitive	*prep.*	preposition
irreg.	irregular verb	*pron.*	pronoun
masc.	masculine	*sing.*	singular

How to find the form you need

Nouns Unmarked nouns ending in -o are masculine; unmarked nouns ending in -a are feminine. Other nouns and exceptions to this rule are marked for gender with the appropriate definite article, **(el)** for masculine nouns and **(la)** for feminine nouns, for example, **tren (el)** and **habitación (la)**.

Plurals The plural form of nouns and adjectives is not included in the glossary. Use this guide to form the plural.
- Nouns and adjectives ending in -o, -a, and -e form the plural by adding -s.
- Nouns and adjectives ending in a consonant other than -z form the plural by adding -es.
- Nouns and adjectives ending in -z form the plural by changing the z to c and adding -es.
- The stress remains the same in the plural as in the singular. Accent marks will, therefore, need to be added or deleted as necessary.

Verbs Unmarked infinitives are regular. The abbreviation (*irreg.*) follows the infinitives of irregular verbs. Infinitives of stem-changing verbs are followed by (o>ue), (e>ie), or (e>i) as appropriate. Examples of these notations are **decir (*irreg.*)**, **almorzar (o>ue)**, **comenzar (e>ie)**, and **repetir (e>i)**.

a un, una, uno
accept (to) aceptar
accident accidente (el)
account cuenta
ache (to) doler (o>ue)
add (to) agregar
adorn (to) decorar
address dirección (la)
after después
afternoon tarde (la)

agency agencia
agent agente (el/la)
advertisement anuncio
air-conditioning aire (el) acondicionado
airline aerolínea
airplane avión (el)
airport aeropuerto
aisle pasillo
allow (to) permitir

alone solo(-a)
already ya
also también
always siempre
American americano(-a)
ancient antiguo(-a)
announcer locutor (el), locutora (la)
another otro(-a)
apartment apartamento
April abril (el)
architect arquitecto(-a)
area code código de área
Argentine argentino(-a)
arrive (to) llegar
art arte (el)
artist artista (el/la)
artistic artístico(-a)
ask (to) preguntar
ask for (to) pedir (e>i)
asleep dormido(-a)
asleep (to fall) dormirse (o>ue)
at en
at one on the dot a la una en punto
at two o'clock a las dos
At what time is ____? ¿a qué hora es
____?
August agosto (el)
available disponible
avenue avenida

bad malo(-a), mal
badly mal
balcony balcón (el)
banana banana
bargain (to) regatear
Baroque barroco(-a)
baseball béisbol (el)
basketball baloncesto
bathroom baño, cuarto de baño
be (to) ser (*irreg.*)
be (to) (in a place or condition) estar
(*irreg.*)
be able (to) poder (o>ue)
be in a hurry (to) tener (*irreg.*) prisa
be right (to) tener (*irreg.*) razón
be sleepy (to) tener (*irreg.*) sueño
beach playa
bean frijol (el)
beautiful bonito(-a), hermoso(-a)

because porque
because of a causa de
become (to) ponerse (*irreg.*)
bed cama
beer cerveza
before antes
begin (to) comenzar (e>ie)
believe (to) creer
bellboy botones (el)
besides además
better, best mejor
bicycle bicicleta
big grande
bill cuenta
blouse blusa
board (to) embarcar
boarding embarque (el)
book libro
boring, bored aburrido(-a)
bother (to) molestar
bottle botella
bracelet pulsera
breakfast desayuno
briefcase maletín (el)
bring (to) traer (*irreg.*)
bus autobús (el)
busy ocupado(-a)
buy (to) comprar
by por

calculator calculadora
call (to) llamar
camera cámara
candidate candidato(-a)
car auto, coche (el)
careful! ¡cuidado!
carry (to) llevar
cash en efectivo
castle castillo
ceiling techo
celebration fiesta
center centro
chair silla
check (to) revisar
cheese queso
cherry cereza
chicken pollo
chicken hash picadillo de pollo
child niño(-a)

Chilean chileno(-a)
chocolate chocolate (el)
choose (to) escoger
church iglesia
cinema cine (el)
city ciudad (la)
clam almeja
class clase (la)
classic clásico(-a)
climb (to) subir
cockroach cucaracha
cold frío(-a)
cold drink refresco
Colombian colombiano(-a)
come (to) venir (*irreg.*)
come back (to) regresar, volver
  (o>ue)
comfortable cómodo(-a)
complete, full completo(-a)
computer computadora
concert concierto
condition condición (la)
cook cocinero(-a)
cool fresco(-a)
correct correcto(-a)
counter mostrador (el)
countryside campo
crab cangrejo
credit crédito
credit card tarjeta de crédito
cropped mocho(-a)
Cuban cubano(-a)
custard flan (el)
cut off mocho(-a)

dancer bailarín (el), bailarina (la)
date fecha
date from (to) datar
day día (el)
December diciembre (el)
delicious delicioso(-a)
delighted encantado(-a)
dentist dentista (el/la)
departure salida, partida
departure gate puerta de salida
desk escritorio
dessert postre (el)
detailed detallado(-a)
die (to) morir (o>ue)

dining room comedor (el)
dinner cena
dinner (to have) cenar
dish plato
dive (to) lanzarse
diver clavadista (el/la)
do (to) hacer (*irreg.*)
doctor doctor (el), doctora (la)
dollar dólar (el)
door puerta
dot punto
dot (on the) en punto
double doble
drink bebida
drink (to) beber, tomar
dry (to) secar
due to a causa de
during durante

each cada
eighth octavo(-a)
electrician electricista (el/la)
elevator ascensor (el)
embroidered bordado(-a)
enchant (to) encantar
engineer ingeniero(-a)
English inglés, inglesa
English (language) inglés (el)
enjoy (to) disfrutar
enough bastante
enter (to) entrar
entrance entrada
excited entusiasmado(-a)
excuse me perdón
exercise (to) hacer (*irreg.*) ejercicio
expensive caro(-a)

factory fábrica
fantastic fantástico(-a)
fall (season) otoño
fall (to) caer (*irreg.*)
fast rápido(-a)
father padre (el)
favorite favorito(-a)
fear miedo
February febrero
feel (to) sentir (e>ie)
feel like (to) tener (*irreg.*) ganas
fifth quinto(-a)

figurine figurita
fillet of hake filete (el) de merluza
finally finalmente
find (to) encontrar (o>ue)
finish (to) terminar
first primero(-a)
fix (to) arreglar
flight attendant auxiliar de vuelo (el/la)
floor piso
food comida
foot pie (el)
for me para mí
forget (to) olvidar
fork tenedor (el)
fourth cuarto(-a)
French francés, francesa
French (language) francés (el)
Friday viernes (el)
fried frito(-a)
friend amigo(-a)
from de, desde
fruit fruta

generally generalmente
gentlemen señores (Sres.)
get off bajar de
give (to) dar (*irreg.*)
glass (drinking) vaso
go (to) ir (*irreg.*)
go down (to) bajar
go out (to) salir (*irreg.*)
go up subir
gold oro
good bueno(-a)
good morning buenos días
good-bye adiós, chao (*informal*)
Gothic gótico(-a)
grilled a la plancha
group grupo
guide guía (el/la)
gym gimnasio

haggler regatón (el), regatona (la)
hair dryer secador de pelo (el)
hairdresser peluquero(-a)
half mitad (la), medio(-a)
hat sombrero
have (to) tener (*irreg.*)

have a good time (to) pasarlo bien
have lunch (to) almorzar (o>ue)
he él
head cabeza
hear (to) oír (*irreg.*)
heat calor (el)
here aquí
himself, herself se
his, her, your, their su
historic, historical histórico(-a)
holy sagrado(-a)
homework, task tarea
horribly horriblemente
hotel hotel (el)
hour hora
house casa
how? ¿cómo?
how are you? ¿cómo estás?
how many? ¿cuántos(-as)?
how much? ¿cuánto?
hunger hambre (el) (*fem.*)
husband esposo

I yo
ice cream helado
idea idea
if si
immediately inmediatamente
impossible imposible
impressive impresionante
in en
in order to para
include (to) incluir
included incluido(-a)
inexpensive barato(-a)
infinitive infinitivo
information información (la)
ingredient ingrediente (el)
intelligent inteligente
interesting interesante
international internacional
interview entrevista
introduce someone (to) presentar
Italian italiano(-a)
ivory marfil (el)

jade jade (el)
January enero

jewel joya
journalist periodista (el/la)
juice jugo
July julio
June junio

key llave (la)
kind amable
knife cuchillo
know (to) (places or people) conocer (*irreg.*)
know (to), know how (to) saber (*irreg.*)

lady señora
language lengua
last último(-a)
last night anoche
late tarde
later luego, más tarde
lawyer abogado(-a)
learn (to) aprender
leave behind (to) dejar
lemonade limonada
less menos
letter carta
lettuce lechuga
library biblioteca
like (to) gustar
like (I) me gusta
like (I would) me gustaría
listen (to) escuchar
literature literatura
little bit poquito
live (to) vivir
lodging hospedaje (el)
lodging (to take) hospedarse
look at (to) mirar
lose (to) perder (e>ie)
loser perdedor (el), perdedora (la)
lost (to get) perderse (e>ie)
love (to) amar, querer (e>ie)
love (I) (an activity) me encanta
luckily por suerte
luggage equipaje (el)
luggage (hand) equipaje (el) de mano
lunch almuerzo

mad (to get) enojarse
magazine revista
make (to) hacer (*irreg.*)
make plans (to) hacer (*irreg.*) planes
many muchos(-as)
March marzo
market mercado
married casado(-a)
marvelous estupendo(-a)
matter (to) importar
May mayo
Mayan maya
me, to me, myself me
mean (to) querer (e>ie) decir
mechanic mecánico
meet (to) encontrarse (o>ue)
menu menú (el)
Mexican mexicano(-a)
midnight medianoche (la)
mine mío(-a)
minute minuto
Miss señorita, Srta.
mix (to) mezclar
mixed surtido(-a)
moment momento
Monday lunes (el)
money dinero
month mes (el)
monument monumento
more más
morning mañana
move (to) mover (o>ue)
movie película
movies (to go to the) ir al cine
Mr., Sir señor, Sr.
Mrs. señora, Sra.
much mucho(-a)
museum museo
music música
must (one) hay que
my mi

nation país (el)
near cerca
necktie corbata
need (to) necesitar
never nunca
news noticias
newspaper periódico

next próximo(-a)
nice simpático(-a)
night noche (la)
ninth noveno(-a)
noodles fideos (los)
noon mediodía (el)
notebook cuaderno
notebook (small) libreta
nothing nada
nothing else nada más
novel novela
November noviembre (el)
number número

October octubre (el)
of course por supuesto
offer (to) ofrecer
office oficina
often a menudo
old viejo(-a)
older mayor
olive aceituna
omelet (Spain) tortilla
on en
only solamente, sólo
open (to) abrir
orange naranja
order pedido
other otro(-a)
our nuestro(-a)
outskirts alrededores (los)
overdo (to) exagerar
owner dueño(-a)

pack (to) hacer (*irreg.*) las maletas
pair par (el)
palace palacio
paper papel (el)
parents padres (los)
park parque (el)
party fiesta
passport pasaporte (el)
past pasado(-a)
pass through (to) pasar por
patron saint patrón (el), patrona
  (la)
pay (to) pagar
peach durazno
pearl perla

pencil lápiz (el)
pepper chile (el)
performance función (la)
Peruvian peruano(-a)
philharmonic filarmónica
piano piano
pineapple piña
play (to) (a game) jugar (u>ue)
play (to) (an instrument) tocar
player jugador (el), jugadora (la)
please por favor
please, do _____ favor de + *inf.*
pleased to meet you mucho gusto,
  encantado(-a)
plumber plomero(-a)
plus más
point punto
police policía
poor pobre
popular popular
portion porción (la)
postcard tarjeta postal (la)
practice (to) practicar
prefer (to) preferir (e>ie)
prepare (to) preparar
prepared preparado(-a)
president presidente (el), presidenta
  (la)
price precio
princess princesa
private privado(-a)
problem problema (el)
professor profesor (el), profesora (la)
program programa (el)
put (to) poner (*irreg.*)
pyramid pirámide (la)

question pregunta

read (to) leer
realize (to) darse (*irreg.*) cuenta
receive (to) recibir
reception desk recepción (la)
receptionist recepcionista (el/la)
recommend (to) recomendar
  (e>ie)
red rojo(-a)
red snapper huachinango
remember (to) recordar (o>ue)

repeat (to) repetir (e>i)
report informe (el)
reservation reservación (la)
rest (to) descansar
restaurant restaurante (el)
return vuelta
return (to) volver (o>ue)
rice arroz (el)
ride paseo
right away ahora mismo, en seguida
roll of film rollo (el) de película
roof techo
room habitación (la)
round-trip viaje (el) de ida y vuelta
rug alfombra
ruins ruinas
run (to) correr
Russian ruso(-a)

sad triste
salad ensalada
salt sal (la)
Saturday sábado
sauce salsa
school escuela
sea mar (el)
seat asiento
seat belt cinturón (el) de seguridad
second segundo(-a)
secretary secretario(-a)
see (to) ver (*irreg.*)
sell (to) vender
separate (to) separarse
September septiembre (el)
serape sarape (el)
serve (to) servir (e>i)
service servicio
seventh séptimo(-a)
she ella
shoe zapato
shrimp camarones (los) (used in Latin America), gambas (used in Spain)
silver plata
since desde
sing (to) cantar
singer cantante (el/la)
single, unmarried soltero(-a)
sit (to) sentar (e>ie)

sitting sentado(-a)
situation situación (la)
sixth sexto(-a)
sleep sueño
sleep (to) dormir (o>ue)
small amount poco
smoke (to) fumar
so much tanto(-a)
so-so más o menos
soccer fútbol (el)
some unos, unas
something algo
something else algo más
sometimes a veces
soon pronto
sorry (I am sorry) lo siento
soup sopa
Spain España
Spanish español, española
Spanish (language) español (el)
speak (to) hablar
speaking of a propósito
special especial
spicy, hot picante
spoon cuchara
spring primavera
square (public) zócalo
stamp sello
steak bistec (el)
stomach estómago
strawberry fresa
street calle (la)
student estudiante (el/la), alumno(-a)
stuffed relleno(-a)
subway metro
suitcase maleta
summer verano
sun sol (el)
Sunday domingo
swim (to) nadar
swimming pool piscina

table mesa
take (to) tomar
take a walk (to) dar un paseo
take along (to) llevar
take pictures (to) tomar fotos
taste (to) probar (o>ue)
tax impuesto

taxi taxi (el)
teaspoon cucharita
telephone teléfono
television televisión (la)
temple templo
tennis tenis (el)
terminal terminal (el)
terrible terrible
thank you gracias
that que, eso, ese(-a)
the el, la, los, las
theater teatro
there allí
there is, there are (*irreg.*) hay
they ellos, ellas
thing cosa
think (to) pensar (e>ie)
third tercero(-a)
thirst sed (la)
this esto, este, esta
through por
Thursday jueves (el)
ticket (round-trip) pasaje (el) de ida
    y vuelta
till I see you hasta la vista
time (as in one time, once) vez (la)
tip propina
tired cansado(-a)
to a
today hoy
tomato tomate (el)
tomorrow mañana
total total (el)
tour gira
touristic, tourist turístico(-a)
towel toalla
traditional típico(-a)
train tren (el)
travel (to) viajar
treasure tesoro
trip viaje (el)
Tuesday martes (el)
TV tele (la)
typical típico(-a)

understand (to) comprender
university universidad (la)
until hasta
us nos

vacate (to) desocupar
vacation, vacations vacaciones (las)
vegetables (fresh) verduras
vendor vendedor (el),
    vendedora (la)
Venezuelan venezolano(-a)
very muy
veterinarian veterinario(-a)
view vista
violin violín (el)
virile macho
visit (to) visitar

waiter mozo, camarero, mesero
waitress camarera, mesera
walk (to) caminar
walk (to take a) dar (*irreg.*) un
    paseo
wall pared (la)
walnut nuez (la)
want (to) querer (e>ie)
wash (to) lavar
wash oneself (to) lavarse
watch (to) mirar
water agua (el) (*fem.*)
we nosotros
weather tiempo
Wednesday miércoles (el)
welcome (you are) de nada
welcome to ____ bienvenidos
    a ____
well bien
what? ¿qué?, ¿cuál?
when cuando
when? ¿cuándo?
where? ¿dónde?
where to? ¿adónde?
whether si
which? ¿cuál?
while mientras
white blanco(-a)
why? ¿por qué?
wife esposa
wind viento
window ventana
window (small) ventanilla
wine vino (blanco o tinto)
winter invierno
wish (to) desear

with con
with me conmigo
with you contigo, con Ud., con Uds.
without sin
work (to) trabajar
work (to) (machines) funcionar
worse peor
worth (to be) valer (*irreg.*)
would like to (I) quisiera

write (to) escribir
write down (to) anotar

yard patio
yes sí
you tú (*fam.*), usted (*formal*), ustedes (*pl.*), vosotros (*pl.*, used in Spain)
younger menor
your tu, su